JESUS, LIBERATION, AND THE BIBLICAL JUBILEE

OVERTURES TO BIBLICAL THEOLOGY

Editors

WALTER BRUEGGEMANN, Professor of Old Testament at Eden Theological Seminary, St. Louis, Missouri

JOHN R. DONAHUE, S.J., Professor of New Testament at the Jesuit School of Theology, Berkeley, California

*Images
for
Ethics
and
Christology*

JESUS, LIBERATION, AND THE BIBLICAL JUBILEE

SHARON H. RINGE

 FORTRESS PRESS   Philadelphia

COPYRIGHT © 1985 BY FORTRESS PRESS

Library of Congress Cataloging in Publication Data

Ringe, Sharon H.
  Jesus, liberation, and the Biblical jubilee.

  (Overtures to Biblical theology ; 19)
  Includes index.
  1. Jesus Christ—Person and offices. 2. Christian
ethics. 3. Jubilee (Judaism) 4. Freedom (Theology)—
Biblical teaching. 5. Bible. N.T. Gospels—Criticism,
interpretation, etc. 6. Bible. O.T.—Criticism,
interpretation, etc. I. Title. II. Series.
BT202.R55 1985   232   85–4609
ISBN 0–8006–1544–1

1736C85 Printed in the United States of America 1–1544

To my parents
Hilda Foehr Ringe
Frank Albin Ringe

Contents

Editor's Foreword

When this series, Overtures to Biblical Theology, was initiated (1977), the most that could be said was that there was an increasing methodological uncertainty in Scripture study. The old and reliable historical-critical methods were increasingly felt to be inadequate, though not obsolete or superseded. The way forward was by no means clear.

The brief period since that time has seen considerable activity concerning fresh methodological possibilities. While there is still a great deal of uncertainty—and therefore diversity—one may safely observe that two methods now claim considerable respect among scholars, a respect that was scarcely visible as recently as 1977.

The first of these is literary criticism—as distinct from the older source analysis. Literary criticism seeks to take the text as it stands and treat it as an offer of a new reality that was not available until the text was presented in just this form. The text creates something new that awaited this particular rendering. Therefore the particular rendering must be observed in close detail. That is, it is *the power of concrete language in particular, concrete form* that is the focus of such study. This kind of investigation has been given impetus by Amos Wilder, Paul Ricoeur, and Sallie McFague.

The second of these more recent methods is sociological analysis, (see Robert Wilson, *Sociological Approaches to the Old Testament* [Philadelphia: Fortress Press, 1984]). This method seeks to understand the text as a statement of social interest reflecting and serving a particular social group, expressing a particular social vision and social agenda. At the forefront of such an analysis are matters of interest, power, and ideology. This approach has attracted the attention of many scholars. In Old Testament (OT) study, reference should be made, in addition to Wilson, to the programmatic work of Norman K. Gottwald. In New Testament (NT) study, especially prominent is the work of John Gager, Wayne Meeks, and Gerd Theissen.

This book by Sharon Ringe is an important "overture" to biblical theology precisely because it makes careful use of these two methods in a discerning juxtaposition to each other. On the one hand, Ringe is attentive to sociological matters. She understands that the Jubilee texts articulate a quite concrete and quite radical social agenda, one that is intentionally transformative and set as a challenge against the social monopolies of the day. This is true in its initial legal setting in ancient Israel. It is also true in its subsequent uses in the Old and New Testaments.

Ringe understands, however, that the continuing power of Jubilee language is not as a legal insistence nor as a didactic proposal. She sees that the *social proposal* of Jubilee has come to function as a *powerful metaphor,* so that what was sociology now takes on literary rhetorical power well beyond a specific social proposal. This means it is no longer a flat social proposal to be implemented or rejected, but it is now a linguistic act that continues to have dangerous power in all sorts of contexts that are neither legislative nor didactic. As a metaphor of dangerous power, it cannot be reduced and contained simply as a social proposal.

The metaphor of Jubilee stays rooted in the ancient social proposal, but it spills over as an imaginative possibility wherever these texts are permitted to have a say. The metaphor now invites to a social possibility that lies well beyond the initial proposal.

One of the enormous gains in this "overture" is a fresh way of relating Old and New Testament texts. The old conventional ways of law-gospel, promise-fulfillment, or typology did not take into account the primal power of textual language itself. This move to break out of these scholastic and predictable categories, Ringe shows, lets the concrete language of Israel continue to have transformative and subversive power when used in new contexts. Such a usage of the OT permits a very different reading of the gospel tradition and its rhetorical and therefore social power.

The second important gain is that Ringe shows how this use of language—*social proposal become liberated metaphor*—can continue to be "read forward" (p. 36). That is, the transference of the metaphor of Jubilee to the NT is not the last such linguistic transference. The metaphor as elusive and evocative social possibility continues to push forward into the life of the community wherever the text is taken seriously.

The combination of these two methods prevents two dangers in our hearing. First, the Jubilee cannot be taken simply as an ancient and outmoded social proposal, because its literary power lets it be poignant even in our new circumstance. Second, the metaphor is not a mere metaphor or a mere literary usage, because the resilient power of Jubilee as social proposal will not let it be so easily dismissed.

Ringe is not skimpy on serious, detailed exegetical matters. But along with that, she shows how the text has power beyond its first hearing. She understands how the text functions in the service of transformative liberation without becoming ideology in any particular way. This is not an essay in method. But Ringe proceeds with methodological intentionality to show what exegetical and expository advances are possible when the text is considered through such new questions.

We are obviously not at the end of our current methodological exploration and clarification. Nonetheless, Ringe's work is an important evidence of how much the field has changed and how greatly new methods permit the text power and authority in relation to new social circumstances and possibilities. When one finishes with the book, one has the sense that the text has had its say in a fresh way. Such exegesis permits us not simply to draw a conclusion, but to continue to listen to wherever else the text will lead the listening community. That text is, as Ringe's way shows, not yet finished with its people.

WALTER BRUEGGEMANN

Preface

This book began with a sermon. The pastor of a congregation on Manhattan's West Side reflected on what might happen to the beleaguered city of New York and its many poor people if suddenly someone declared a Jubilee. The images of Leviticus 25 began to haunt me, and I found myself drawn into the study of their history and subsequent interpretation in Hebrew Scriptures and in the Gospels of the NT. In the process of that study, I learned something about the power of images to shape human life, and about Jesus Christ as the herald of liberation.

This book grew along with my commitment to liberation in a world where people are oppressed because of their race or sex or politics, and where the poor must struggle merely to live. My own journey into feminism has helped me to learn also from people involved in other liberation movements in this country and in Africa, Asia, and Latin America. As I have wrestled with the implications of the various agenda of liberation, the images found in the Jubilee traditions have given them shape and grounded them in the very core of the biblical faith. This book presents an exploration of those images, and of their significance for Christology and Christian ethics.

The place to begin is Luke's account of Jesus' rejection at Nazareth, where the following words from the Book of Isaiah are linked to Jesus:

> The Spirit of God is upon me, for God has anointed me to preach good news to the poor. God has sent me to proclaim release to the captives

and recovery of sight to those who are blind, to set at liberty the
oppressed, to proclaim the acceptable year of God. (Isa. 61:1–2a,
quoted in Luke 4:18–19)

This Word of God fulfilled in the presence of Jesus of Nazareth is
alive with images of liberation. From their origins late in Israel's exile,
where they addressed the people's longing for political freedom and
for the healing of a shattered society, these images continued to be
words of blessing and hope to people living in occupied Palestine in
the first century of the Common Era. For the early church, these
same images defined Jesus' public ministry. They answered once for
all the question, "Are you the one who is to come, or shall we look for
another?" (Matt. 11:3//Luke 7:19). The images we glimpse in this
opening portrait from Luke's Gospel are spun out in greater detail in
the stories, sayings, parables, and prayers contained in the Synoptic
Gospels. Together they present Jesus as a royal messenger announcing the "good news" of liberation at the beginning of God's reign.

Both the content and the pattern of this proclamation are rooted in
the Jubilee and sabbath-year traditions of Hebrew Scriptures (Exod.
21:2–6; 23:10–11; Deut. 15:1–18; Jer. 34:8–22; Isa. 61:1–2), and in
the royal edicts of release found in records of societies that were
Israel's neighbors. In these traditions liberty is presented in economic, social, and political terms: freedom for slaves, release for
captive peoples, cancellation of debts, redistribution of land, care for
the poor, food for the hungry, and healing of physical ailments. The
language is primarily the language of ethics, dealing with values,
social relationships, and the establishment or restoration of justice.

Two factors transform and enlarge this Jubilee language as it finds
its way into the gospel traditions. First, images that began in social,
political, or economic spheres are associated with God's eschatological reign. Just as that reign is at once physical and spiritual, social and
individual, political and personal, so the Jubilee declared at its incep-
tion touches all of human life. We are never given a blueprint for
God's reign, but in the Jubilee images we get a glimpse of those points
of intersection where daily life of human design encounters the truth
of God's sovereignty.

Second, the Jubilee traditions become sources for the language of
Christology as well as of ethics. Jesus as the Anointed One (Christ/
Messiah) of God is presented as the herald announcing the beginning
of God's new reign, and proclaiming liberty to all who participate in

it. To portray Jesus as the herald of God's reign is to emphasize Jesus' intimacy with God, for a royal messenger would be accorded the same dignity as the sovereign who is represented. To portray Jesus as the proclaimer of the Jubilee links recognition of Jesus as the Christ with response to the Jubilee message itself: to confess Jesus as the Christ is to participate in acts of liberation.

This study of the role of Jubilee images in ethics and Christology is predicated on two related methodological points. The first has to do with the imagistic nature of christological language. The second has to do with the social and cultural sources of images and with their political consequences: Christology and ethics are intertwined. Those methodological points, then, provide a hermeneutical key for reflecting on the implication of Jubilee images for Christology and ethics in contemporary contexts. The methodological discussion also stretches this study beyond its specific focus on the Jubilee traditions in the Gospels, to become the basis for an examination of the ethical implications of other christological confessions contained in the church's tradition.

It is my hope, then, that the evidence set forth in this study of the intimate connection between the agenda of liberation and the core of the Christian faith will support persons and groups who are involved in contemporary liberation struggles. I hope also that the methodological points that are made will contribute to the crucial discussions of contextual theology and hermeneutics going on in both church and academy.

Scripture quotations are my own translations unless otherwise indicated. They represent my effort to render the texts in inclusive English.

I am indebted to the faculty and Board of Trustees of the Methodist Theological School in Ohio for the faculty fellowship that supported my work on this book, and to Andover Newton Theological School for their hospitality to me as visiting scholar during my sabbatical leave.

My exegetical work on the Jubilee passages owes much to the assistance I received from members of my dissertation committee at Union Theological Seminary: Raymond E. Brown, Walter Wink, James A. Sanders, Phyllis Trible, and Donald M. Shriver, Jr.

My colleagues Jeffrey Hopper and Everett Tilson have helped me clarify many of the theological and hermeneutical points in the discussion. I am very thankful for their help and especially for their friendship.

Walter Brueggemann's support, encouragement, and guidance have been crucial to my work through all the stages of the development of this manuscript. Everyone should have such an editor for one's first book! In addition, Harold W. Rast, John A. Hollar, and their colleagues at Fortress Press have been most gracious in their guiding of this book through the final stages of publication.

I am particularly grateful to students whose enthusiasm and probing questions have lent energy to my work. It is for these students, and for any others who might be helped by it, that this book was written.

Engagement with the agenda of liberation takes seriously one's context and pulls one toward the future. It also leads one to recognize one's history and roots. For that reason, this book is dedicated to my parents.

Sharon H. Ringe
Methodist Theological School in Ohio

Abbreviations

AGJU	Arbeiten zur Geschichte des antiken Judentums und des Urchristentums
BA	*Biblical Archaeologist*
B.C.E.	Before the Common Era
BDF	F. Blass and A. Debrunner. *A Greek Grammar of the New Testament and Other Early Christian Literature.* Trans. and rev. R. Funk from the 9th–10th Ger. ed. Chicago: Univ. of Chicago Press, 1961.
CBQ	*Catholic Biblical Quarterly*
EncJud	*Encyclopaedia Judaica.* New York: Macmillan Co., 1971.
ExpTim	*Expository Times*
Gos. Thom.	*Gospel of Thomas*
HUC	Hebrew Union College
IEJ	*Israel Exploration Journal*
Int	*Interpretation*
JANESCU	*Journal of the Ancient Near Eastern Society of Columbia University*
JAOS	*Journal of the American Oriental Society*
JB	Jerusalem Bible
JBL	*Journal of Biblical Literature*
JJS	*Journal of Jewish Studies*
JSOT	*Journal for the Study of the Old Testament*
KJV	King James Version of the Bible

LXX	Septuagint. Greek translation of the Hebrew Scriptures
NovT	*Novum Testamentum*
NT	New Testament
NTS	*New Testament Studies*
OT	Old Testament
P. Oxy.	*Oxyrhynchus Papyrus*
1QH	*Hôdāyôt (Thanksgiving Hymns)* from Qumran Cave 1
1QM	*Milḥāmāh (War Scroll)* from Qumran Cave 1
11QMelch	*Melchizedek* scroll from Qumran Cave 11
1QS	*Rule of the Community (Manual of Discipline)* from Qumran Cave 1
1QSa	Appendix A (*Rule of the Congregation*) to 1QS
RelSRev	*Religious Studies Review*
RSV	Revised Standard Version of the Bible, 1973 ed.
TDNT	G. Kittel and G. Friedrich, eds. *Theological Dictionary of the New Testament.* Grand Rapids: Wm. B. Eerdmans, 1964–74.
TS	*Theological Studies*
TToday	*Theology Today*
UBSGNT	United Bible Societies' *Greek New Testament*
USQR	*Union Seminary Quarterly Review*
VT	*Vetus Testamentum*
ZNW	*Zeitschrift für die neutestamentliche Wissenschaft*

CHAPTER 1

The Language of
Ethics and Christology

Images and Social Context

The purpose of this study is to explore the sources, development, and implications of the Jubilee images found in the Synoptic Gospels. Before turning to the biblical material, however, we must examine in a more general way the nature of christological language and the relationship between such language and the historical, cultural, and social contexts in which it occurs.

METAPHOR, PARABLE, AND SYMBOL: FINITE LANGUAGE AND TRANSCENDENT REALITY

People characteristically think, speak, and learn in pictures, stories, and analogies.[1] We approach what is unknown by looking for similarities to and differences from what is known, and by noting ways they are alike and not alike at the same time. Children explore new worlds by finding ways to relate what is unfamiliar to familiar things and spaces. The zebra and lion in the new picture book are "sort of like" the horse and cat in its well-thumbed predecessor. The water in the huge lake is not totally unlike that in the bathtub or wading pool. Even abstractions like numbers, directions, or values are learned by comparison or contrast with others, or are explicated in specific, concrete analogies or stories. We know what "up" means from having been lifted to the shoulders of a very tall grandfather, and we know "down" as the place where we can scurry about on our own after being held too long on someone's lap. Many of us learned what "perseverance" means from "The Little Engine That Could." As we grow, we forget the source of such learnings in concrete experiences. When an adult tries to learn a new language, or explores a new culture, or seeks to comprehend a new political crisis, however, the process of learning by reference to familiar experiences, places, or ideas begins again.

If stories, pictures, and analogies are facts even of the most commonplace aspects of our lives, especially at points of learning or transition, they are even more vividly part of our attempts to think and speak of experiences or values dearest to us. The closer we come to the center of our lives, the less language is able to say what we mean in a direct, literal way: ask someone what "love" means, and sooner or later you will hear a story. We point toward that which gives life and energy to us, instead of analyzing or defining it, as though we dare not name it too precisely lest we violate that toward which we reach. We touch delicately what awe or fear or need or love forbids us to grasp.

When we attempt to speak about God, we are dealing with that which is both central to our lives and ultimately beyond our experience. It is particularly true, therefore, that in our speaking about God, we can only point toward God by stories and pictures that both *are* and yet *are not fully* the truth about God, about the vastness and unconditionality of God's love, or about God's intent for humankind: "The realm of heaven is like leaven which a woman took and hid in three measures of meal, till it was all leavened" (Matt. 13:33). Only by such strong yet gentle speech can we confess the God who transcends all we could ever say about God, and yet is most intimately present in our lives, and only by such speech can we hold open a space for the richness of God's continuing relationship with humankind to unfold.[2]

It is difficult to know what to call the language that is especially appropriate to matters at the core of human life. Literary critics and philosophers of language have suggested such terms as "metaphor," "parable," and "symbol" as the general label. In their discussions of these terms, they point to essential qualities of such language, but none of these terms alone seems adequate.

Metaphor

A "metaphor" is a figure of speech in which a name or descriptive term is transferred to some object different from but analogous to it.

Although the strict, literary sense of this term is too restrictive, the "expressive" power of metaphors is more broadly characteristic of the sort of language we are seeking to describe.[3] A metaphor is not merely a vivid illustration of a general quality that could be presented as well or better by a concept or literal description. Such a restatement would say at once more and less than the original metaphor, and hence cannot be considered to be of equivalent cognitive significance.[4] Instead, by its linking of unlike but somehow analogous terms, a metaphor is at once true and untrue. In the tension between truth and untruth, a metaphor expresses a unique aspect of, perspective on, or feeling about the object.[5]

For example, an encyclopedia or a zoology textbook would provide adequate descriptions of the large, striped cat we call "a tiger." Some but not all of those descriptions would be relevant to an understanding of what it means to call a person "a tiger." Such a metaphor suggests both a number of qualities exhibited by the person so described and something about the relationship between the subject and the object. The nature of those qualities and that relationship can be probed or examined or elaborated, but they can never be precisely restated or translated into literal language. Similarly, to call God "Father" does not mean that God is one's male parent, but it does suggest qualities both recognized in God and present in the relationship between God and the believer. Those too are not immediately, literally clear, but need to be probed, examined, and elaborated. To call God "Father" is no mere illustration, but rather in its complexity and in the tension between truth and untruth, it too expresses something about God that can be precisely communicated in no other way.

Parable

"Parables" share with metaphors this expressive, and not merely illustrative, function. At a basic level, parables are metaphors expanded through time in a narrative form. The brief stories attributed to Jesus in the Synoptic Gospels are paradigms of this type of language. They are not illustrations of various theses about God's reign, such that once the thesis is discovered the story becomes superfluous. Instead, each story, with its particular historical and cultural color and its carefully crafted details, highlights and alludes to a cluster of interrelated aspects of the nature of God's reign encountered in human experience. The episodes of the story function not to impart information, but rather to confront the hearer or reader by their unpredictable patterns of behavior and sequences of action, such that the story itself becomes an experience of the nature of God's reign.[6]

The point of interpreting a parable is not that the hearer should be able to understand it in an intellectual sense. Rather, the interpreter seeks to introduce the hearer to the situations depicted in the parable and assumed by its earliest audiences, so that its impact can be experienced afresh. The hearer can then be reoriented in and toward her own life situation as she finds herself siding with one character or another, or taking a stand toward the particular event that the parable sets forth. In that reorientation she can then catch a new glimpse of what God's reign is like.

What, for example, is being said about God's reign by the parable of the leaven cited above (Matt. 13:33)? No data are conveyed, but one is confronted with the daily task of bread baking, and in the pondering of that task various details come into focus. One is immediately aware of the contrast in amount of working leaven and inert dough, and of the hiddenness of the leavening process. One is at least subliminally aware that the leavened dough is a live organism, and not an inert product of human action or creation. The finished bread serves to nourish people at a most basic level of their lives. The whole episode is drawn from household experience and what then was women's work. It centers on a substance, the leaven, which was banned from ritual cereal offerings (Lev. 2:11; 6:17), and banned from every household during the holy season of Passover (Exod. 12:14–20). Such details are jarring when juxtaposed with the holiness of God's reign. In fact, they run counter to people's usual notions of what is appropriate to a "reign," and to normal human perceptions of power and majesty. To speak of God's reign by means of such a story communicates to the hearer both something about the nature of God and something about the relationship of the speaker to God. In receiving the story, the hearer is addressed, confronted, and perhaps transformed.

Symbol

"Symbol" is a third term appropriate to some of the linguistic, artistic, and literary devices in the broader category of language we are considering. Norman Perrin defines a symbol as "a primary intentionality which gives second and subsequent meanings analogically."[7] Speaking of symbolic language, Paul Ricoeur observes,

> all symbolic language is a language which says something other than what it seems to say, and by its double meaning, releases meaning, releases signification. And in the same way, it plays the role of an exploratory instrument of my existential possibilities, of my situation in being.[8]

Both "symbol" and "myth," which Ricoeur and Perrin describe as a symbol developed in the form of narration, address on the second and subsequent levels of meaning matters beyond perceptual experience. In the very act of verbalizing or otherwise expressing such matters, symbols not only name meanings that already exist, but also evoke new meanings. Symbols give rise to thought.[9]

Symbols too serve both to conceal and to reveal that to which they refer. From a perspective informed by but distinct from the depth psychology of C. G. Jung, Phillip Wheelwright calls a symbol "that which means or stands for something more than (not necessarily separate from) itself, which invites consideration rather than overt action, and which characteristically (although not perhaps universally) involves an intention to communicate."[10] Elsewhere he defines a symbol as "a relatively stable and repeatable element of perceptual experience, standing for some larger meaning or set of meanings which cannot be given, or not fully given, in perceptual experience itself."[11]

Wheelwright distinguishes among several types of symbols. First, there is the basic distinction between "tensive symbols" and "steno symbols" or "signs" (such as road signs) whose meanings are shared in the same way by a large number of people. Tensive symbols can then be divided into several types. "Symbols of ancestral vitality" are borrowed by an author from earlier written sources. "Symbols of cultural range" evoke meaning and references to the broader traditions of a particular culture, historical community, or religious body. The "reign of God," with its many echoes in the literature of Hebrew Scriptures, would be such a symbol in the Jewish and Christian communities. Finally, "archetypal symbols" are those, like bread or water, that carry power and similar though not necessarily identical meanings for all or most human beings.[12]

"IMAGES" AS THE ENCOMPASSING TERM

These brief comments about metaphor, parable, and symbol point toward the sort of language that is appropriate for speaking of a transcendent reality, and thus appropriate language for Christology. Even these categories taken together, however, do not include the full range of qualities that mark such language. As a more inclusive term, I would suggest "images." Images can be understood to exhibit several characteristic qualities.

1. *Images form reality.* They express and thereby create the world in which one's action takes place. The limits of the language or images at one's disposal set the limits of one's world. For example, the vocabulary and syntax of patriarchal language entail an entire structure of relationships, both between person and person, and between person and God.

2. *Images are rooted in particular social, cultural, and political contexts.* This rootedness works in two directions. First, the images that are most powerful in one's life are drawn primarily from the stories, rituals, geography, experiences, and expressions of value of one's own culture, and secondarily from one's study, reading, or other transcultural exploration. They are thus not neutral but "interested," and represent a structure of value and meaning that is operative in one's life. Second, images not only *reflect* but also *form* the context of one's life. The images with which and by means of which one speaks and thinks become part of one's political, social, economic, cultural, and religious identity.

3. *Images have the power to change one's world.* Like the parables of the Synoptic Gospels, images in general can shape one's vision and reorient one's life by the way familiar ingredients are combined and reordered to challenge predictability and inertia. We are caught by the image in the juxtaposition of familiar and strange, the one luring us in, and the other confronting our lives. Images can be the provokers of initial cracks in preconceptions, making clear the limiting political consequences of our prior vision of the world, and moving us toward action and transformation as our perceptions change. There is no "innocent eye" of the perceiver, for who one is affects one's perception, but then when perception changes, one ceases to live or move or act in the old world.[13]

4. *Images are tensive and elastic.* They undergo changes as they are

perceived, and as people respond to them. When they are told and retold, parables acquire various accents, and metaphors attract elaborations that highlight various aspects of the perceptual as well as the referential subject. Images are not static, but organic. They evolve, grow, bear fruit, and spawn other images. When they outgrow their bounds, they die or are transformed into something harder or more static, such as "signs" (Wheelwright) or "models" (McFague). Insofar as the Bible presents its traditions by means of and in the form of images, the authority of the Bible must be understood in a way that is not rigid or literalistic, but that itself embodies tension, dialectical patterns, openness, growth, and relativity.[14] In that sense, Walter Brueggemann calls the authority of the biblical story an "active" authority that conveys the faith by engaging both the listener and the teller in communication which is "a bonding around images, metaphors, and symbols that are never flattened to coercive instruction."[15] The purpose of the story, then, is neither to command nor to communicate information, but to evoke the imagination.

5. *Images bridge traditionally separate fields of inquiry and arenas of life.* This integrative function of images is related to their tensive or elastic quality. McFague observes,

> the most fruitful metaphors are the ones with sufficiently complex grids to allow for extension of thought, structural expansion, suggestions beyond immediate linkages. Thus, in this sense, "liberator" is a good metaphor for God because it entails a complex structure for thought which can be elaborated.[16]

To speak of God or of Christ as liberator is immediately to draw in aspects of human experience, patterns of relationship, and political, economic, and social as well as personal and soteriological dimensions of life. Because of its complexity, the image will not stay narrowly confined into a predefined meaning for human life. Instead, it engages the imagination, evoking responses whose final consequences cannot be easily predicted or controlled. In Brueggemann's analysis, this creative, integrative function of images underlies the power of prophetic poetry "to take Israel *inside* the life-experiences which might be treated *externally* as only ethical or political," and to claim "that the texture of human suffering and human healing is a match for what happens in the heart of God."[17]

6. *Images must be interpreted.* This interpretation is a process

requiring but not limited to intellectual investigation of meaning, and careful use of historical and literary critical tools. The latter are necessary because of the cultural and historical relativity of images which requires that they be examined in their own contexts and, as much as possible, in the terms of their early users. Furthermore, the fundamentally literary quality of the images demands that one understand how language, style, and literary form are related to meaning. The interpretation of images, however, is not the one-way street, with clear identification of subject and object, that the critical paradigm seems to presuppose. Rather, there must be what McFague calls an interaction of hearer and images which are "texts." Common interests initially open up the texts. Eventually, however, it is the "reader" who is questioned by the texts, with the result of a merging of horizons of text and reader. When that happens, the interpretation is more an amplification than an analysis, and it creates a "third point of meaning" beyond where either the reader or the text began.[18] When the task of interpretation relates to the biblical traditions, and particularly to the proclamation of God's reign, McFague affirms that *"to be a believer is to be on a continuum with being human."*

> To be a human being is to interpret, to think of "this" as "that," to make judgments concerning similarity and difference, to think metaphorically. To be a believer is to follow the way of the parables and Jesus as parable, to live with the tension between the kingdom and the world, never identifying the one with the other while aware of the transformation of the world by the kingdom.[19]

Thus the task of interpretation is finally not an academic undertaking, but a style of presence in the world. It too is in the realm of ethics, which must be understood to include living with imagination, living with the images of our confession about God and about the Christ.

CHRISTOLOGY AS ETHICAL CONFESSION

Like all images, the images by which one confesses the Christ are historically and culturally relative. That relativity is evident on two levels. First, the cultural matrices and historical traditions undergirding the confessing community as a whole have influenced the pool of available images by which the Christ might be confessed. That pool, which initially would seem vast and inclusive, has been limited by events and institutional considerations that have resulted in some images being seen as useful or acceptable to the concerns of the church, while others are ignored or even condemned. In this process, images such as those prominent in the various "heretical" sects of the early church were lost for many centuries, only to be recovered later under the influence of historical inquiry. Conversely, as the Christian faith has taken root among people in Asia, Africa, and native communities of the Americas, the pool of available images by which to express the meaning of "the Christ" has grown. All of the images, however, bear the mark both of a particular context in which they emerged, and of the cultural, historical, and ecclesial traditions through which they have passed.

In addition to reflecting the broader historical and cultural range of the confessing community, images of the Christ also reflect the specific social, political, and historical circumstances of the particular confessor or segment of the confessing community. This second level of the relativity of those images accounts for the particular images that rise to prominence at a given place and time.[20] Thus, certain images from the larger pool of available images might be set aside because, due to scientific discoveries or changes in technology, social patterns, or world view, the old images no longer communicate at all, or even begin to make a point opposite to that which they originally made. At other times old images are dismissed because they communicate a dimension of the Christ deemed troublesome or even unacceptable to the community or its leadership. Political and ecclesiastical criteria thus might account for the decisions in the early church about the tolerable limits of heterodoxy,[21] just as they underlie both enthusiasm for and rejection of the work of theologians of liberation today.

The selection among the variety of images available in the church's tradition reflects the particular ways fundamental issues about human life are encountered. Not only universal human concerns, such as awareness of our mortality and concern about the meaning of life, but also immediate factors related to one's place in the political structure, economy, and society affect the way one will speak about the Christ. For example, the systemic facts of racism, sexism, classism, militarism, and colonialism, and our commitment to support or to overturn them, become embedded in the images by which we talk about the one in whom God's redemption of humankind is present. In short, one's Christology implies one's ethics. As Rosemary Radford Ruether observes,

> one's portrait of Jesus ultimately expresses one's own normative state-
> ment about the Christian message to the world today. If there is no
> connection between these two, then there is indeed no need to continue
> to speak of Jesus as the Christ or the Gospels as Scripture.[22]

The biblical traditions regularly present God's gracious act on behalf of humankind as the context and pattern for human life. Torah is first of all recitation of the core stories about the covenant people, and only in the context of that recitation do we find the canons for human behavior. Grace and law are thus inseparable, and the way the first is formulated sets the terms for how the second is perceived. In the NT context, this means that Christology is the foundation for ethics.[23]

To say that Christology is the foundation for ethics, however, does not mean that one's moral life is to be normed by the imitation of Christ or of the pattern of Jesus' life presented in the Gospels and known through critical study. The connection between ethics and Christology is more subtle and more intimate than that. The key to the way in which the two are joined is the integrative capacity of the images by which the Christ is represented. These images function not to persuade one of the greater reasonableness or logic of one course of action over another, but rather to establish the contours of the world in which one's action takes place. They set those contours either by presenting a coherent picture of the central reality and consequent dimensions of one's life, or by upsetting the predictable play of events and relationships by putting the pieces of one's life together in new ways.

The constitutive or conservative function of images in Christology has predominated in the evolution of church tradition and doctrine. As people have sought ways to make the audacious claim that in the human being Jesus, God's ultimate intent for humankind is known, images accenting the transcendent, otherworldly aspects of the Christ have multiplied. At times they have all but eclipsed images accenting the essential fact that this one called the Christ was human as we are. The accent on the otherworldly and transcendent dimensions of the Christ has its parallel in the devaluing of physical, historical life, and in the denying of the importance of one's involvement in the activities and choices of the secular political, social, and economic world. Under this influence, salvation has been regarded as a matter affecting only the soul and determined by the life of one's spirit, rather than intimately connected with the public, political, and social dimensions of one's life.

This "idealist" trend in Christology, which is mirrored in one's hermeneutic and other phases of theological reflection as well, leads to the building of what Ruether calls "hierarchical models," in that they undergird existing patterns of dominance and oppression.[24] In such models, both Christ and the Christian message are presented as apolitical and otherworldly. These qualities represent choices favored by people who are the winners and beneficiaries of political, social, and ecclesial controversies, and for whom the existing systems of society and of the community of faith function well. On the other hand, these hierarchical models, with their political and other ethical consequences, carry negative implications for the oppressed.

In these models, Christ is no longer the bearer of "good news to the poor" since the models support the status quo, quietism, and the pretense of detaching questions of salvation and faith from doing justice. In fact, the Christ portrayed in such models becomes the sanction for evil. A part of one's probing of the images of Christology, then, must include both the unmasking of such models and the search for "revelatory paradigms by which to construct a redeeming vision of an alternative humanity and world."[25] The focal point for such a critical and transforming vision, Ruether suggests, is in the teaching and liberating action of Jesus. At that point, Ruether clearly aligns herself with other theologians of liberation for whom the Jesus who walked the roads of first-century Palestine, rather than the Christ of the church's proclamation, is the focus of christological confession and ethical reflection.[26]

IMAGES, HISTORY, AND PROCLAMATION

A methodological difficulty is introduced by the insistence of many theologians of liberation, as well as of many evangelical and fundamentalist Christians, that one ground one's christological confession as well as one's ethics in the historical Jesus. That difficulty consists in the fact that critical study of the Gospels makes it clear that their authors did not intend to provide neutral, factual information about Jesus. From glimpses of the perceptions of Jesus by his contemporaries, through the post-Easter memory of the early church, the Gospel writers present proclamations of Jesus as the Christ and testimonies to a power recognized as God-with-us. It is of course true that the earliest materials are less adorned with the colors and treasures of the church's iconography, which moved increasingly away from Jesus' humanity in order to accent the intimacy of his relationship with God. Nevertheless, even in the earliest materials the stress is not on factual accuracy but on clearly accented and stylized pictures. Those pictures relate what it meant that the Jesus who had taught and ministered, who died and was alive again, was the Anointed One (Christ/Messiah) of God.

Even for those who push us toward the "historical Jesus," however, what proves to be important is not producing irrefutable evidence to support particular facts. Rather, what concerns them are the human truths embodied in the perceptions of the person Jesus of Nazareth— perceptions that may include more or less accurate memories of his words and deeds. What matters is the clear memory of Jesus' life as marked by openness to and advocacy for the outcast, and by participation with the poor, the sick, and the dispossessed at their points of greatest pain. The authority of these stories about Jesus lies not in their factual accuracy but in the authority of a particular human life that continues to address people in new circumstances, evoking from them and from us a response to the one confessed as the Christ.

Changes in both methodology and perception are necessary if one is to adapt the traditional disciplines of historical and literary criticism to the task of probing the images in which the gospel story is presented. Elisabeth Schüssler Fiorenza has suggested that a focus on narratives and the particular actors and situations involved in them is an important corrective to the preoccupation of many source and form critics with the sayings found in the gospel traditions. Attention to the historically representative characters and circumstances presented in the narratives allows the stories as well as the sayings and words to be understood in the context of the social-historical world that they evoke.[27] The point is not to secure irrefutable data about Jesus' life, but rather to recognize within their cultural matrix both the sayings and words, and the related perception of Jesus as the Christ, that the text is intended to convey.

The details of the stories by which Jesus is presented as the Christ are not coincidental. Not only do they ground the confession in a particular historical and cultural context, but they also are combined in story form in a way that confronts our human situation with transformative power. We encounter that power not in a blueprint or prescription that is copied or filled, but in the response evoked from us. In responding, we are placed in that newly named world which by its vividness replaces the old perception of reality with which we have lived. We then can act according to that new world, not because we can be sure of particular facts of Jesus' life, but because of who the person Jesus is portrayed to be as the Christ of God. In short, the gospel stories with their vivid details function as the parables do, and in turn they present Jesus as a parable of God.[28]

To speak of Jesus as the Christ in imagistic or parabolic language is to speak theocentrically, and not christocentrically, since to speak of the Christ is to speak of one who is transparent to God. Christians confessing the Christ in the parable of the life of Jesus of Nazareth are saying that in that specific human life we come to know God as we do in no other place. Looking at Jesus, we learn about God's own concern for the poor and dispossessed, God's hospitality to the outcast, and God's style of sovereignty that inverts our usual ways of thinking about power and authority. Under this sovereignty, the rich no longer lord it over the poor, nor do the powerful trample the powerless, nor do the chosen people claim precedence over those who are strangers or aliens. Parabolic language used to talk about the Christ thus reveals God by focusing on the world as it is transformed by God.[29]

These images function as prototypes, not in the sense of patterns to be copied, but as first statements begging to be reformed, re-imaged, and transformed as they intersect our own lives. We are not commanded by the historical Jesus, nor are we given a model to copy or a leader to follow woodenly. Rather, we glimpse God's nature and a statement of God's truth, will, and presence in light of which we can and must now act. "Jesus Christ the Proclaimer of Liberty" is itself an image that evokes clusters of additional images pointing to a truth about God's will and about the institutions and structures of our human society. Because of what we learn about the Christ, we recognize those institutions and structures as penultimate, and allegiance to the Christ means that the power of those institutions over us, and through us over others, has been broken. We in turn are set free to participate with the Christ and with the poor, the oppressed, and the disenfranchised of our world in struggles for liberation.

JESUS AND THE JUBILEE: PROBING
IMAGES OF LIBERATION

The christological and ethical reflections of theologians of liberation present a particular challenge to those of us in the faith communities and theological academies of the so-called First World. For theologians of liberation, biblical images of liberation speak with a power and directness that come from the intersection of these images with the experiences and struggles of oppressed peoples. If there is a danger to the perception of such immediate connections, it is that these images risk being translated in a literal fashion, to coincide with political and social programs recognized as urgent for the contemporary society. For us, on the other hand, the problem is that our own social location among the privileged muffles the images of liberation, so that we fail to be grasped by them, or else we recognize only those dimensions of the images that do not threaten us. We have to work at opening up the images themselves, and at understanding their historical and social contexts as well as our own, in order to experience the power of those images again.

What follows in this study is an example of the probing of one cluster of images that present Jesus Christ as Liberator—namely, the ones associated with biblical Jubilee traditions. The first two steps in the study involve the amplification of those images using the tools of historical and literary criticism to examine both the contexts in which those images emerged and were reinterpreted and the literary function of the images in the passages where they occur. First, the Jubilee traditions found in Hebrew Scriptures are examined in order to present a fuller picture of their origins, connotations, and theological implications. Second, the recurrence and further interpretation of those traditions in the Synoptic Gospels are explored with particular attention to the circumstances in which they appear to have been associated with Jesus as well as to their christological and ethical consequences. Finally, these same images are played against concerns and questions arising in the contemporary context, in some initial suggestions of how the Jubliee images continue to address us.

We cannot help but see the images associated with the Jubilee from our own perspective or standpoint. That standpoint is also the only place where we can, and therefore where we must, participate in the struggles that define our own lives and those of our sisters and brothers. Our yearnings and theirs for justice and peace—yearnings to be free, to be safe, to be warm and fed, to be healthy and whole—frame the questions we address to the one we confess as the Christ. From the depths of the traditions of the community of faith we learn that the Christ is one in whose company the hungry are fed, the sick healed, the outcast embraced, and the fearful comforted, and we learn that crucial to any confession of Christ is action to free the poor from entanglements that impoverish and enslave. Through these images of the one who as the Christ heralds the Jubilee of God's reign, we might find the courage to struggle for justice and peace, and to dare to yearn for the time of liberty acceptable to God.

CHAPTER 2

Jubilee Traditions
in Hebrew Scriptures

A Cluster of Images

The pageantry of trumpets and the declaration of "liberty" set the contours of the biblical Jubilee. The festival and its social consequences are set forth in Leviticus 25:

> And you shall count seven weeks of years, seven times seven years, so that the time of the seven weeks of years shall be to you forty-nine years. Then you shall send abroad the loud trumpet on the tenth day of the seventh month; on the day of atonement you shall send abroad the trumpet throughout all your land. You shall hallow the fiftieth year, and proclaim liberty throughout the land to all its inhabitants; it shall be a jubilee for you, when each of you shall each return to your property and each of you shall return to your family. (Lev. 25:8–10)

Interspersed throughout the rest of that chapter are regulations concerning the redistribution of real estate, the cancellation of debts, the freeing of slaves, and the designation of an agricultural fallow year. Marking each of these regulations is a concern for social justice, not as charity, but as liberation. Undergirding all of them is language that acclaims God as sovereign over the people themselves and over all creation.

Although Leviticus 25 is the focus of a discussion of the Jubilee, that chapter is more appropriately the midpoint than the beginning of such a discussion. Two strands of Israel's tradition come together in Leviticus 25. The first of these is made up of sabbath-year laws (Exod. 21:2–6; 23:10–11; Deut. 15:1–18). These laws, which regulate the repayment of debts and establish an agricultural fallow year, recognize a connection between such social responsibility and the worship of God who is at once sovereign in and liberator of Israel. The second strand of tradition contributing to the Jubilee laws of Leviticus 25 consists of various royal decrees of amnesty or "release" found in the surrounding culture of Mesopotamia as well as in biblical stories (Jer. 34:8–22; Neh. 5:1–13). These decrees further accent the connection between confession of God as sovereign and obedience to laws requiring social justice. A review of these two strands of tradition prepares the way for an examination of Leviticus 25 and of the prophetic expression of the Jubilee in Isaiah 61.

The biblical Jubilee traditions occur in a variety of literary forms and in material stemming from diverse historical circumstances. Each of these traditions needs to be investigated in its own social and historical context in order for its particular implications to emerge. Not only do the images in which these traditions are cast not always carry the same connotation, but there is no neat trajectory showing a development from one to another. Instead, the Jubilee traditions are related to one another in their affirmation of God's sovereignty and their mandating of deeds of justice and liberation.

THE SABBATH-YEAR LAWS: LEGISLATIVE FORERUNNERS OF THE JUBILEE

The Covenant Code

The oldest of the biblical laws underlying the Jubilee are part of the Covenant Code (Exodus 21—23). This collection of laws governing the religious and social life of Israel has been incorporated into the Exodus narrative at the point of the Sinai theophany, where they elaborate on the Israelites' obligations to the God who had initiated a covenant with them. The "treaty" form of this covenant foundation of Israelite life places God in the role of the monarch of Israel, just as the narrative context affirms that the same God is Israel's liberator.

The conjunction of these two images of God suggests a social context prior to the establishment of Israel's monarchy. Unlike its neighbors, which had basically monarchical forms of government, early Israel appears to have followed a less centralized and less hierarchical pattern of social organization. In fact, Norman Gottwald has suggested that it was precisely Israel's egalitarian social structure that represented the strongest challenge to surrounding societies, and that led to the success of the Israelites in establishing themselves as distinct social groups in the land of Canaan. He concludes, "In Israel *as a polity or realm of self-rule,* Yahweh is the ultimate and sole *sovereign,* the surrogate king, who guarantees the diffusion and de-centralization of power within the several sovereign groups of the community."[1] Thus, the Israelite notion of divine sovereignty por-trayed God as actual ruler over the people and over the society, and contained few of the metaphysical interpretations of divine sov-ereignty common among Israel's neighbors. This different notion of divine sovereignty, in turn, appears to have had its roots in God's redeeming action on behalf of Israel that is portrayed in the Exodus story, and its consequences for the people in the obligations that form the laws of the Covenant Code.[2]

The two portions of the Covenant Code that are most closely related to the Jubilee are Exod. 21:2–6 and 23:10–11. In these laws, the means by which God is confessed as sovereign and liberator is portrayed as involving the freeing of slaves and the granting of a "rest" for the land. In the first of these texts, the term "Hebrew," with its complex history, points to the relationship of these laws to Israel's own saga of liberation. In the second, the theme of God's sovereignty is elaborated in the context of Israel's life as an agricultural society.

Exodus 21:2–6 does not speak of a particular sabbath year or of a general emancipation of slaves, but rather of the proper treatment of individual "Hebrew" slaves. The word "Hebrew" is problematic, since it may refer to people who are aliens in a particular land, or to those with the status of slaves.[3] With either meaning, it would be an appropriate word to denote the position of the Israelites in Egypt. Whatever its original meaning, in Exodus 21 the term is equivalent to "Israelite." The Hebrews or Israelites are people forced into the extreme measure of selling themselves and their families into inden-tured servitude in order to obtain money with which to pay living expenses. The laws recorded in Exod. 21:2–6 provide for the release of such persons, and in certain cases of their families as well, after six years of service.

Several factors point to the primitive nature of the provisions in Exod. 21:2–6. First, the release of each person is calculated from the date when service began, rather than on the basis of a time of release commonly observed throughout the society. Second, those released move into a halfway status in which they are partially dependent on the people they served since there is no provision for them to be given any capital to protect them against falling right back into debt again. Third, the provision for the ear-piercing ritual which marks the permanent status of a slave who refuses manumission is portrayed as a cultic act presupposing the existence of many local sanctuaries to which the slave might be brought. These factors, plus the emphasis on individual kindness and compassion without reference to any impact on social organization, suggest that these laws concerning the release of slaves may have come from a time when Israel was just beginning to discern the ethical consequences of its experience of Yahweh the sovereign liberator.

Exodus 23:10–11 introduces the agricultural fallow year that was to be observed every seventh year. Again, there is no clear reference to a commonly observed sabbath year in which all cultivated land would be idle. It is not even clear whether all of the land of a particular farmer would remain idle at one time, or whether some system of crop rotation is envisioned. In any event, the purpose of the fallow year is humanitarian: those who do not own land are allowed to harvest crops produced spontaneously by it in the years when it is not cultivated. The larger context of the chapter accentuates the social, economic, and humanitarian motives and implications of this legislation. For example, Exod. 23:6 calls for justice for the poor, and Exod. 23:9 enjoins against the oppression of those who are "strangers" in Israelite society, just as the Israelites themselves were strangers in Egypt. Similarly, Exod. 23:12 establishes the seventh day as a day for the entire household to enjoy rest and refreshment.

The rationale for the legislation throughout Exodus 23, including the laws relating specifically to the agricultural fallow year, is found in 23:9 (RSV): "You shall not oppress a stranger; you know the heart of a stranger, for you were strangers in the land of Egypt." That rationale grounds the legislation in the religio-historical self-understanding of the Israelites. It is their experience of liberation at the hand of God that is the basis of their subsequent actions, and these actions in turn are their expression of allegiance and obedience to the God who is sovereign over them.

Deuteronomic Code

The representation of Torah in Deuteronomy reflects several changes in the life of Israel which suggest that the law has been

interpreted for a more settled, urban society with a centralized political structure. In fact, it is likely that the Deuteronomic Code was
compiled during the reign of Manasseh (687–642 B.C.E.). In the reign
of Josiah (about 621 B.C.E.) a book of the law that may indeed have
been the Deuteronomic Code became the basis for sweeping reforms
(2 Kings 22—23). The laws related to the "release" in the seventh
year illustrate the sort of changes represented in that code, and
suggest the changes in the underlying social context that appear to
have occurred.

In Deut. 15:1–18 there is no specific mention of the agricultural
fallow year, but the terminology of "release" and the reference to a
seven-year period link the collection of laws to Exod. 21:2–6 and
23:10–11. The revised versions of these sabbath-year laws contain
several points that are a commentary on the impact of these laws and
on their social management. Deuteronomy 15:1–18 is composed of
three major sections each declaring from a different perspective the
need to care for the poor. The first section deals with release or
cancellation of debts (Deut. 15:1–6), the second with lending to the
poor (Deut. 15:7–11), and the third with procedures for freeing
Hebrew slaves (Deut. 15:12–18). The picture underlying these laws is
of a society under jurisdiction of a central administration and with a
fairly complex economy. By the time of the codification of laws
represented in Deuteronomy, the term "Hebrews" had come to identify a portion of the population who were able to hold as slaves or
indentured servants both other Hebrews and members of the surrounding society. Since it appears also to have been easy to dis-
tinguish between "Hebrews" and other members of the society, the
term probably had come to identify the ethnic community of Israelites rather than an economic class.

In the laws of Deuteronomy 15, a distinction is clearly drawn
between kinfolk whose debts are released in the seventh year and
foreigners from whom payment can still be exacted.[4] It is not clear,
however, whether the debts even of the kinfolk are actually cancelled
or merely suspended during the year of release. A simple one-year
suspension would fit logically with the provision in Exodus 23 for a
one-year suspension of profit-taking from a farmer's land. Foreigners
not bound by that suspension could still be expected to meet payments as usual, whereas Israelites could not be held to their normal
obligations. This interpretation would make Deut. 15:1–6 an instance

of enabling legislation, adapting the Covenant Code to a period of transition from an agricultural setting to a more urban, commercial one.

Deuteronomy 15:7–11 casts serious doubt on that interpretation, however, since these verses suggest that a mood of tight credit would prevail because of the release of debts. That mood would make sense only if debts were actually cancelled throughout Israel in a commonly observed sabbath year. Deuteronomy 15:9 points to a situation in which a lender faced the prospect of no return, not merely a delayed return, on an investment. Furthermore, the juxtaposition of Deut. 15:7–11, which clearly assumes the continued existence of the poor, with Deut. 15:4–5, which forecasts an end to poverty, implies that the laws were in fact not being observed, perhaps because of their revolutionary, uncompromising effect on business as usual. In addition to the internal evidence in Deut. 15:7–11, later rabbinic interpretation of the laws concerning release of debts also points to a cancellation of debts and not merely to deferred payments. The device of the *prôzbûl,* which established a means for placing debts in escrow to allow their future collection, would have been unnecessary if a total cancellation of debts were not meant.[5]

Closely related to the cancellation of debts is the release of slaves discussed in Deut. 15:12–18. These slaves were really indentured servants whose condition was the result of the debtor and the debtor's family being the security for a loan. The language and content of Deut. 15:12–18 clearly reflect the provisions of Exod. 21:2–6 but with modifications. First, the slaves are not to be released empty-handed, presumably to fall directly back into slavery as soon as they try to obtain credit again. Instead, they are to be supplied with animals and food with which to begin their lives again. Second, in Deut. 15:12 women are specifically included in the release, and are not simply included in the transaction with a man as is implied in Exod. 21:3–4. Third, the symbol of permanent servitude (piercing the ear) has become a secular, economic action, and is not tied to a local sanctuary. That change may well reflect the centralization of the cult and the closing or at least official disapproval of the local sanctuaries. As in the earlier laws in the Covenant Code, however, the timing of the freeing of slaves seems tied to each person's term of service rather than to a universally observed year, despite the contrary practice with respect to the cancellation of debts called for in Deut. 15:1–6 and

7–11. This inconsistency in Deut. 15:12–18 suggests that, although these laws display thematic unity, they are not woven into a single uniform corpus.

As in the case in Exodus 21, the experience of divine action on which human action is modeled is Israel's redemption from slavery in Egypt (Deut. 15:15). Just as that experience, coupled with a firm conviction that Yahweh alone stands as sovereign over Israel, under-girds the laws of the Covenant Code, so also that experience is recalled to anchor the legislative reform of a human king in the precedent of God's rule over Israel. Deuteronomy 31:9–13 again emphasizes that the new law code in general, and the laws concerning the year of release in particular, are linked both to the rule of the king and to the royal sanctuary. According to that instruction, at the Feast of Booths in each year of release the law should be read before the entire people who would have assembled "before Yahweh your God at the place which God will choose" (Deut. 31:11).

ROYAL PROCLAMATIONS OF "RELEASE"

Decree of Zedekiah

The Book of Deuteronomy both contains examples of sabbath-year laws and is itself an example of legislative reform instituted by a king. As such, it represents a transition to the second strand of tradition that appears to underlie the Jubilee laws of Leviticus 25, namely, royal proclamations of release. The ambivalent position of Deut. 15:1–18 is even more evident when one considers the decree of Zedekiah reported in Jer. 34:8–22.

According to the story in Jeremiah, in the time of crisis when the army of Babylon was at the door of Jerusalem (approximately 588 B.C.E.), King Zedekiah heeded the warning of the prophet Jeremiah. In the face of impending defeat, the king would accomplish two things by agreeing with the people to invoke the law concerning the "liberty" of Hebrew slaves. First, he would prove the people's faithfulness to their covenant with God, and thus assure God's protection of them. At the same time, he would accomplish the practical goals of replenishing the ranks of the army for the fight against Babylon, and avoiding having to feed a large slave population during a siege. The agreement was short-lived, however, lasting only as long as the threat of siege, after which time the slaves were taken back by their former owners. This renewed disobedience, not by oversight but by deliberate decision, is identified by Jeremiah as grounds for the indictment of Israel and for the proclamation of their "liberty" to suffer pestilence, famine, exile, and destruction.

The language with which Jeremiah reports God's indictment of the people when they renege on their agreement parallels that of Deut. 15:12. If that law had not been observed for a long time (Jer. 34:14), all the individual times of release would have been long overdue. The agreement that Zedekiah worked out with the people represents not the renewed mandate of a practice to occur every seven years, however, but a single instance of a royal decree effecting the release of all the slaves in the society. Furthermore, the word for "liberty" *(dĕrôr)* in Jer. 34:8 and 17 is not the word one would expect from the legislation cited, where the release is called a *šĕmittâh*. The language of *dĕrôr* instead links the account of Zedekiah's decree to the second major strand of traditions underlying the Jubilee legislation of Leviticus 25, namely, the tradition of royal decrees of amnesty found in the records of Israel's neighbors.

Royal Decrees of Amnesty

The word *dĕrôr,* which is the word for "release" or "liberty" in Lev. 25:10; Isa. 61:1; Jer. 34:8, 15, 17; and Ezek. 46:17, corresponds to Neo-Assyrian and Akkadian words meaning "to move about," "to run away," "to be free," "to become free," or "to be at large."[6] These words occur in the secular documents of Israel's neighbors with two principal references. First, the related Akkadian words are found in legal documents from the ancient kingdom of Hana forbidding by royal decree the permanent transfer of real estate. These decrees include a formula reminiscent of Ezek. 46:17, where the *dĕrôr* is invoked to prevent the giving of royal land to a servant.

Second, these words for "release" referred to the freeing of people from slavery occasioned by extreme indebtedness. In the law code of Hammurabi, for example, there is a reference to the release of a defaulting debtor's wife and children who had been forced to work for the creditor. In similar language, the law code of King Lipit-Ištar of Isin (1937–1927 B.C.E.), whose ancestors came from Mari, established general amnesties in which many people found their terms of servitude simultaneously ended. Court records of Hammurabi, of his son Samsu-iluna of Babylon (1749–1712 B.C.E.), and of his great-grandson Ammi-ṣaguda (1646–1626 B.C.E.) show that near the beginning of each of their reigns similar decrees of "release" were issued. These records indicate that the rulers considered it their duty not only to free those people who had sold themselves into slavery, but also to enable the poor to recover the lands from which economic necessity had separated them.

Except for their specific provisions concerning real estate, the tone and intent of these royal decrees have much in common with the sabbath-year regulations of Israel's Covenant Code and Book of Deuteronomy. The royal provenance of these decrees also mirrors the relationship of the biblical legal codes to Israel's covenant with the God whom they knew first as literally sovereign over Israel, and subsequently as the authority behind the earthly monarchs of Israel and Judah. These similarities appear not to be coincidental. To begin with, the territories where these royal decrees were promulgated had large Amorite populations and were ruled by dynasties of Amorite descent. Given the prominent role played by the Amorites in Palestine during the second millennium B.C.E., it is likely that the Israelites learned of these decrees, recognized the similarity between the decrees and the sabbath-year laws, and associated the particular language of "release" in the decrees with the actions of a royal figure. Furthermore, by the time of Zedekiah, Judah had been a vassal for more than a century, first to the Assyrians and later to the Chaldeans. Those relationships would easily account for Zedekiah's adoption of the pattern of a royal decree when he sought to reinstitute the covenant requirement of the periodic release of Hebrew slaves. It may indeed be the case that the form of a royal decree and the word *děrôr* to express "release" were first joined to Israelite religious laws concerning the sabbath year by the editor of the account in Jer. 34:8–22, whether that editor was Jeremiah himself or a member of the Deuteronomic school.[7]

Decree of Nehemiah

The fact that Israel continued to link such decrees of amnesty to royal figures late into its history can be seen in Neh. 5:1–13. This passage is part of the collection of lists, records, documents, and other materials dating from the rebuilding of the wall around Jerusalem during the administration of Nehemiah at the time of Israel's return from exile. The specific problem being addressed is the practice of usury. Nehemiah 5:10–13 reflects Nehemiah's revulsion at the selling of kinfolk into slavery, which appears to have resulted from such lending practices. Nehemiah's decree, which requires the cancellation of debts for which persons and property are surety, is not grounded in any sabbath law, but in the requirement to honor God and to do what is right, and hence not give the Gentiles reason to think ill of the Jews (Neh. 5:9). There are, however, significant thematic parallels between that passage and the laws collected in Leviticus 25. Those common themes include concern about the practice of lending at interest, the restoration of real estate to its proper owners, the cancellation of debts, and a concern for the fate of the poor, all of which are set in the context of a decree or proclamation of "release." The terminology of *děrôr* is not actually present in Nehemiah, but the decree is issued by Nehemiah acting in his authority as governor and representative of Artaxerxes I, so it is in fact a royal decree of amnesty.

THE JUBILEE IN LEVITICUS 25: DIVINE SOVEREIGNTY AND LAWS OF "RELEASE"

> You shall hallow the fiftieth year, and proclaim liberty throughout the land to all its inhabitants; it shall be a jubilee for you, when each of you shall each return to your property and each of you shall each return to your family. (Lev. 25:10)

The word for the "liberty" that is declared is *děrôr,* which clearly links this passage to the various royal decrees examined above. That word is joined to the word *yôbēl* as a double description or name of the event. The word *yôbēl,* however, presents problems for interpreters. In Exod. 19:13 and Joshua 6, it seems to be the word for a ram's horn, possibly an earlier synonym for *šôpār,* for which the same Greek word *salpix* is often used. If that is its meaning in this passage, *yôbēl* would seem to refer to the instrument by which the celebration was proclaimed. Particularly if one keeps in mind the association of this event with a royal release, the image of blowing a ceremonial trumpet seems appropriate. On the other hand, the verb *ybl* can also be understood to be the root of this word, particularly since the LXX word *aphiēmi,* meaning "bring back," appears to refer to a gradation of meanings of this word. In that case, the Hebrew words *šěmittâh* and *děrôr* would be synonyms of *yôbēl,* and those synonyms would have been used by the redactor to explain both the obscure term and the institution underlying it.

Leviticus 25 is the one biblical text that spells out the legal provisions of the Jubilee. Particular provisions of its laws echo those of the sabbath-year laws discussed above, and its language of "release" links it to the various royal decrees of release. No earthly sovereign is assumed, however, but God's sovereign possession of the land joins God's liberation of Israel from captivity in Egypt as the reason why these laws must be obeyed (Lev. 25:23, 42–55). Just as the laws of Exodus 21 and 23 assume God as the actual covenanted ruler of Israel, so in Leviticus 25 the sovereign God is the royal owner of the land who alone can determine its distribution. Because God is the true owner, any transaction between people can involve only the product of the land, and only those divisions of the land understood to have been mandated by God have lasting validity.

Leviticus 25 includes several types of laws, and probably at least as many layers of composition. The laws specifically related to the Jubilee are of several formal types, including both apodictic and case law, and are found sprinkled among materials of widely differing content. All of these segments together allow one to begin to see the full ramifications of the release that is to characterize the Jubilee: Lev. 25:8–10a deals with the manner of calculating and proclaiming the Jubilee; 25:10b and 13 speak of a return to property and family; 25:11–12 announces an agricultural fallow year; 25:14–17 and 23–28 regulate the sale and redemption of real estate, while 25:29–34 deals with the special case of land in Levitical cities; 25:39–43 and 47–55 mandate the redemption and liberation of kinfolk who have sold themselves into slavery, and thus by implication also mandate the cancellation of the debts that have necessitated the sale.

This disparate collection appears to be made up of pieces of ancient material from several periods, probably woven together as part of the Holiness Code by a priestly editor of the late exilic or postexilic period.[8] The new compilation would resolve a major problem accompanying the people's return from exile, namely, the allocation and subsequent management of the land. The priestly compilers of the laws thus would not only have established their own authority over the regulation of the land and its inhabitants, but at the same time would have legitimized their administration by a reaffirmation of its basis in God's sovereignty. The religious sanction that such legislation would have lent to their authority would have been crucial in the consolidation of their power and in the establishment of the holy and righteous people under God which was their aim.

If they had actually been observed, the collection of Jubilee laws would have had a sweeping impact on the social and political life of any community governed by them. The scope of that impact can be seen by several points of comparison with the sabbath-year laws. First of all, the Jubilee laws are public, general laws affecting the whole country at once, and not private contracts between creditor and debtor, as is the case in Exod. 21:2–6 and Deut. 15:1–18. Second, the laws in Lev. 25:47–54 provide for the release of those indentured to non-Israelites, which the sabbath-year laws do not. The command to return to the land of one's ancestors, which is not found in any of the underlying sabbath-year laws, marks another significant difference between the laws in Leviticus and those in Deuteronomy and Exodus. Like the laws concerning the release of slaves, provisions for a return to one's land imply the cancellation of debts. With the restoration of real estate, however, the former debtor could hope to attain economic independence instead of merely beginning a new cycle of poverty and indebtedness. Thus, even though the Jubilee years and the concomitant social upheavals would be further apart than the sabbath years of release, their more dramatic consequences would make the Jubilee years even more difficult for the wealthy to observe. In fact, one must ask whether the Jubilee was ever actually observed, and if so, how often.

The legislation itself is unclear about whether the Jubilee was intended to be a repeated event or a single occurrence. Leviticus 25:15 implies a cyclical pattern of Jubilee years, since the value of land is to be calculated according to the number of years after the previous Jubilee. Elsewhere in the chapter, one looks forward to a Jubilee that might indeed be a one-time redistribution of the land following the occupation or, perhaps more accurately, the return from exile.[9] This ambiguity concerning the number of Jubilees may reflect the origin of the Jubilee traditions in both the cyclical sabbath-year laws and the royal decrees of release that carry no pattern of regular repetition, and that appear to have occurred only once in the reign of any sovereign.

The words *yôbēl* and *dĕrôr*, which are characteristic of Jubilee texts, shed little light on such questions. Of the two citations in Hebrew

Scriptures in addition to Leviticus 25 where the word *yôbēl* refers to a Jubilee observance, one (Num. 36:4) seems to refer to a single Jubilee, and the other (Lev. 27:17–18, 23–24) points to a repeated event. Ezekiel 46:16–18 does not refer to a yôbēl year but to a year of liberty *(děrôr)*. That passage also refers to a repeated event involving a general regulation of the prince's distribution of the inheritance in the time after Israel's return from exile. On the other hand, the *děrôr* proclaimed by Zedekiah and recorded in Jer. 34:8–22 was a one-time event. With Leviticus 25 and Isaiah 61, these are the only biblical references where the word *děrôr* means "release." In two of the remaining three occurrences of the word, Prov. 26:2 and Ps. 84:3, it refers to a bird, and in Exod. 30:23 it is generally translated as "liquid" (RSV, JB) or, following the LXX, "pure" (KJV).

Historical accounts and records similarly fail to clear up the mystery surrounding the observance of the Jubilee. Neither Hebrew Scriptures, nor the intertestamental literature, nor secular accounts mention the observance of a Jubilee year in any part of the Jewish community. The argument from silence would suggest, therefore, that whatever the intent of these laws, they were not enacted as part of public policy. Surely if there had been as far-reaching an economic and social revolution as that which would have ensued from the observance of a Jubilee, it would not have gone unnoticed. The actual role of the Jubilee laws in Israelite society is difficult to assess. The redactors of the Holiness Code, like the priests and other official leaders, appear to have approached the problems of Israel's resettlement by concentrating on the concrete ordinances and judgments that would prepare the way for God's dwelling in the midst of the people.[10] The Jubilee laws are significant in that, in the very midst of the Holiness Code with its emphasis on cultic matters, these laws bear witness to the continuing power of the image of God as sovereign over Israel, and to the fact that such an image of God has ethical consequences. To confess God as sovereign includes caring for the poor and granting freedom to those trapped in a continuing cycle of indebtedness. God's sovereignty is presented as a fact bearing on people's daily life and structuring their relationships with one another and with the rest of the created order.

PROPHETIC AMPLIFICATION OF
THE JUBILEE

The writings of Third Isaiah represent a different response to the circumstances of the end of the exile and the need to restructure life in the community that had returned. As Paul Hanson points out, there is "a unified eschatological ideal running throughout the material," making clear its roots in the writings of Second Isaiah.[11] Among the visionaries from whom these writings derive, a longing for God's imminent glorification of Zion takes the place of a concern for the day-to-day rebuilding of the city that is seen, for example, in the writings of Ezra and Nehemiah. The oracles of Third Isaiah present an inclusive understanding of the holy people, in contrast to the hierocracy envisioned by such representatives of the official political and cultic leadership as the editors of the Holiness Code or the writers of the prophecies of Haggai and Zechariah. The program of reform and action presented by Third Isaiah is sketched in impressionistic poetry rather than in prosaic detail. In the face of the political and economic ascendancy of the hierocratic group, what was initially seen by the visionaries as a radical tension between the concretely historical and the mythical dissolved, and God's redeeming intent for the people was projected further and further from the realities of everyday life.[12]

Isaiah 61:1–2

The oracle found in Isa. 61:1–2 gives evidence that Jubilee imagery was as much at home in the poetry of the visionaries as in the legislation of their rivals:

> The spirit of the sovereign Yahweh is upon me,
>   for Yahweh has anointed me
> to proclaim good news *(bśr)* to the poor
> and has sent me to bind up the brokenhearted,
>   to proclaim liberty *(děrôr)* to the captives
>   and the opening of the prison to those
>   who are bound,
>   to proclaim the year acceptable to Yahweh
>   and a day of vengeance for our God,
> to comfort all who mourn.
>   (Isa. 61:1–2)

The oracle represents a message to be delivered to the people concerning the establishment of God's eschatological reign. The message is marked by several themes or general concerns as well as by specific images, all of which are woven together into an intricate structure. These images have their roots in oracles of Second Isaiah,[13] and in Psalm 146 where God is depicted as creator and as the sovereign who carries out the royal obligation of doing justice among the people, as well as in the Jubilee traditions found in Leviticus 25.

The finite verbs in the sentence, "(he) has anointed" and "(he) has sent," are completed by a series of infinitives of purpose depicting the events that are to mark the beginning of God's reign. Four principal images are used to convey the content of these events. The first three—good news to the poor, comfort to the brokenhearted, and release to captives—are linguistically uncomplicated. The fourth is more problematic. The verb *pqḥ*, used here for "opening the prison," refers elsewhere in the Bible only to "opening the eyes" (or the ears in Isa. 42:20). This unusual usage is complicated by the addition of the word or particle *qôaḥ* whose grammatical function and meaning are obscure. Indeed, ancient as well as modern interpreters have puzzled over the construction as can be seen by the fact that in the ancient versions and in modern translations the phrase is translated sometimes as "the opening of the prison" and at other times as "the opening of the eyes." Since Isa. 42:7 and at least one secular inscription[14] use the metaphor of "opening the eyes" as a way of talking about liberation from prison, the mixing of images in Isa. 61:1 may have been intentional. The blending of images in the fourth purpose clause, and their combination with those in the first three, leads to the conclusion that the beginning of God's eschatological reign is to be marked by the proclamation of a "release" from all the experiences of enslavement or imprisonment that characterize human life.

Although there are many points of similarity between this oracle and the Servant Songs of Second Isaiah, a new element has been added to characterize the time favored by God. That element is the setting at liberty *(dĕrôr)* of the oppressed. Just as the language used in the oracle to speak of "release" is the same as that found in Leviticus 25 *(dĕrôr)*, so also the event portrayed in the oracle is the proclamation of a royal edict of release on behalf of the divine sovereign whose reign is at hand. The proclaimer of the message is defined not by any personal identity or power, but by the bearing of the message in which the divine will is both spoken and effected.

The question of the identity of the speaker of the oracle is both difficult to resolve and crucial for the interpretation of the passage. On one level, the passage appears to be an account of the call and commissioning of the prophet who is the unknown author called Third Isaiah. The link thereby established between the role of prophet, the fact of anointing, and endowment with the divine spirit, plus the description in the Hebrew text (but not found in the LXX) of the prophet's being "sent" *(šlḥ)*, establishes the prophet as a messenger from God.

Two additional factors support the importance of the role of messenger in this passage. The first is the traditional link of the language of revelation in prophecy with the mythological role of the messenger of the divine council. That this role is in fact associated with prophecy in Israel can be seen in 1 Kings 22:5–28; Psalm 82; Isa. 6:1–12; 35:3–4; 40:1–18; 48:20–21; 57:14; Jer. 23:18; and Zech. 3:1–10.[15] The second factor is the use of the verb *bśr* to name the messenger's principal task. The participial form of this verb (in Greek *euaggelizomenos*) is also used to designate the herald who appears in Isa. 40:9; 41:27; 52:7. As both prophet and "herald," the speaker is clearly God's messenger, and consequently one who draws all necessary authority from the sender. In Isa. 61:1–2, insofar as the sender is the sovereign God, the messenger is a royal herald who brings the good news of the advent and imminent enthronement of Yahweh.

Finally, the role of the "servant of God" must be joined to those of prophet and messenger or herald in order to fill out the dimensions of the speaker of this oracle. The similarities of basic message and of actual wording between this oracle and the Servant Songs support the joining of this enigmatic figure to the others, even though the servant is not described as being "anointed."[16] The servant's authority, like that of the prophet and the messenger, derives from the one served and not from the human person or community bearing the title. In other words, all of the titles that come together in this passage make it clear that all power and authority are God's. They point to the future as God's future, and to a theocentric instead of an anthropocentric locus of future hope.[17]

It is clear that God is the source of both the authority of the speaker and the hope underlying this passage. It is also clear that what is envisioned is not merely a historical event such as the return of the Jews to Palestine, but the advent of God's eschatological reign. Nevertheless, the visionaries who produced the passage make it clear that the consequences of what is hoped for are experienced in the institutions of everyday life and the attributes of the created order. In Isa. 61:1–2, as indeed throughout Third Isaiah, social and political institutions whose oppressive power is broken are highlighted as the place where God's transformative intent is manifest. Although "new heavens" and a "new earth" summarize the promise (Isa. 66:22), that newness must take root in human deeds and choices. In the midst of the optimism of the return to the land, and of the myriad details confronting the people as they sought to rebuild their society, the visionary community carried on the themes and concerns of Isaiah and his exilic follower (Second Isaiah). In so doing, they celebrated God's commitment to justice and concern for the poor and suffering, and the requirement that people confess their faith in God by showing that same commitment and concern.

CONCLUSION

Throughout the history of Israel, from the early sabbath-year laws in the Covenant Code to the interpretations of the late Second Temple period,[18] traditions associated with the Jubilee appear to affirm two things. The first is that God is sovereign over Israel, both in actual fact and in eschatological hope. The second is that the structures of economic and social life must embody the people's affirmation of God's sovereignty. In other words, God's reign and humankind's liberation go hand in hand. The language of Isa. 61:1–2 proved particularly helpful in sustaining that dual affirmation in the latter part of the Second Temple period, and indeed came to play the same role in that reform movement within first-century Judaism which formed the basis of Christianity.

CHAPTER 3

Jesus as
Herald of Liberation

*Jubilee Traditions Cited
in the Synoptic Gospels*

The Jubilee traditions found in Hebrew Scriptures are rich in images of political liberation, economic reversal, and social revolution. Those images in the various historical and social contexts of ancient Israel made and continue to make significant claims about God and about the ethical consequences of being the people of God. Similarly, those images in the Synoptic Gospels made and continue to make significant claims about Jesus as the Christ and about the ethical dimensions of discipleship. Discovering what those claims might be for the various Gospel writers, for the early church, and for Jesus' own ministry, as well as for us, requires that we begin by identifying criteria for recognizing Jubilee images in the Gospels, and then that we critically examine the relevant pericopes to see in what social, political, and ecclesiastical contexts they appear to have functioned.

RECOGNIZING JUBILEE IMAGES
IN THE GOSPELS

At the very outset, it is important to realize that by asking about the occurrence of Jubilee images in the church's interpretation of Jesus as the Christ, we are asking questions that would not have occurred to the Gospel writers or to those who told and collected the underlying stories and teachings. Such questions lead us to analyze phenomena in the end product of their work, rather than to struggle as they did with how to assemble and accent their material in order to present an appropriate picture of Jesus as the Christ. In that sense, we and the Gospel writers are approaching the Gospels from opposite directions.

The constructive task of those who formulated the Gospels involved drawing together the church's memory of Jesus' life and teaching. That memory included both information about events or sayings of Jesus and reflection on the significance of that information. Among the categories and criteria brought to bear on that reflection were references to Hebrew Scriptures, and, as Greek came to be the common language of the church, to their formulation in the Septuagint. In this interweaving of information and interpretation, factual accuracy was a concern secondary to the concern for clarity about what led them to see this Jesus as the Christ. Similarly, scriptural traditions were introduced not for their own sake, but for the purpose of communicating the theological significance of what Jesus had said and done, and the implications of the resulting confession that this was the Anointed One (Christ/Messiah) of God. This christological purpose must be kept in mind in evaluating any claim to find references in the Gospels to traditions from Hebrew Scriptures.

The task becomes more complicated when the traditions one is investigating are the Jubilee traditions. In Hebrew, Jubilee traditions are marked by a special vocabulary, notably the word *děrôr* (and occasionally the word *yôbēl*) to mean "release" or "liberty." In Greek, however, the vocabulary is not distinctive or peculiar to Jubilee traditions. Thus, for example, in the LXX of Lev. 25:10 and elsewhere, both of those Hebrew words are rendered by the common word *aphesis*, which has a broad range of meanings beyond the Jubilee traditions.

Since there is no distinctive Greek vocabulary associated with Jubilee traditions, one must begin the search for those traditions in the Gospels by looking for places where Jubilee texts are actually quoted or closely paraphrased. Thus, the quotation of Isa. 61:1-2 in Luke 4:18-19 and its paraphrase in Matt. 11:2-6//Luke 7:18-23 establish a basis for claiming that at least that particular Jubilee tradition is actually present in the Gospels. These passages, in turn, provide a context in which to understand particular images and themes found in the text from Isaiah as they occur elsewhere in the Gospels. Because of the lack of a specific Greek vocabulary related to the Jubilee, one ought to be very cautious about claiming to find references in the Synoptic Gospels to Jubilee traditions not actually quoted or paraphrased, such as Leviticus 25.[1] Once the presence and significance of Jubilee traditions in the Gospels have been established on the basis of texts actually cited, possible references to other associated traditions might be noted. They should not, however, be given as much weight in one's argument as would be given to passages containing references to texts known to be among the resources drawn upon by the Gospel writers.

The fact that common Greek words are used to present the Jubilee traditions means that one must be careful not to cite one phrase or image by itself, and then draw the conclusion that Jubilee traditions are indicated. As noted above, for example, it would be wrong to assume that every mention of the word *aphesis* is evidence of a Jubilee tradition, and it would be equally wrong to conclude that every reference to "proclaiming good news" is a citation of Isa. 61:1. Similarly, while the affirmation of a sovereign God is characteristic of the Jubilee traditions, they are by no means the only locus of that affirmation in Hebrew Scriptures. On the other hand, one is on stronger ground in claiming the presence of Jubilee traditions on the basis of a cluster of several of those terms or images occurring in a single passage, or in the same source or collection of materials underlying the Gospels (Mark, Q, or the special Lukan or Matthean sources).

Even when one has proceeded with the greatest possible care in identifying Jubilee traditions in the Gospels, questions about the motives, intent, or purpose of the Gospel writers, the early church, or even Jesus himself cannot be answered with certainty. One simply cannot know for certain whether these traditions were incorporated because they are Jubilee traditions, or because of particular points which they make (such as the proclamation of good news or the declaration of *aphesis*). If questions of motive are elusive, however, questions of meaning and importance are clear. Once one has determined at what level of the formation of the Gospels these traditions were introduced, one can look at them against the background of that and subsequent periods in the life of the early church. Those various social, political, and ecclesiastical contexts provide clues to the meaning and impact of the images by means of which the Jubilee traditions are presented, and to the ways in which their liberating power, and the portrait of Jesus as the herald of liberation, were either blunted or affirmed.

At its very root, the Jubilee is about liberty. Using Isa. 61:1–2 as a base, one finds that three principal images come together to characterize the Jubilee: the announcement of God's reign by one anointed by the Holy Spirit to be a messenger, the proclamation of good news to the poor, and the declaration of "release" from captivity to various forms of imprisonment and enslavement. Both the messenger and the message point to the boundary moment when allegiances are to be shifted from the structures, systems, and institutions that characterize the old order, to the new Sovereign whose reign is at hand. Rather than giving a blueprint for what God's reign will be like, or signs by which it can be recognized, or clues to the time when it will begin, the Jubilee traditions point to what happens whenever humankind encounters the fact of God's sovereignty.

The details of that encounter have varied in different times and circumstances, as have the ways in which these aspects of the portrait of Jesus as the Christ have been related to the larger christological discussion of the church. The images in which the Jubilee traditions are cast continue to express the dynamics of that encounter as they address us in our contemporary context. For us, the critical disciplines and questions that we bring to the study of the ancient texts and societies become part of our context, just as do our social, political, economic, and cultural identities. We are therefore addressed by the Jubilee traditions both in ways consistent with their original framing and in ways independent of and even foreign to it. The power of these images to help us say what it means to confess Jesus as the Christ, as well as to confront our assumptions concerning values and priorities in our daily lives, becomes a vehicle by which we read forward or interpret from the biblical traditions into our own situation.

THE REJECTION AT NAZARETH
(LUKE 4:16–30)

The clearest reference to any of the Jubilee texts in the Synoptic Gospels is the quotation of Isa. 61:1–2 and 58:6 in Luke 4:18–19.[2] That quotation must be understood both in its general context, as part of Luke's introduction to Jesus' public ministry (Luke 4:14–44), and in the particular context of the account of Jesus' rejection at Nazareth (4:16–30). The analysis of these contexts must be carried out in two steps. First, both the rejection pericope and its place in the Lukan narrative must be examined to see to what extent the components of those pericopes shed light on the way the quotation from Isaiah is being interpreted. Second, since the account would have borne different meanings in different social, political, and ecclesiastical contexts, it is important to attempt to determine at what level of the formation of the Gospel the account may have originated.

The Lukan Context of the Rejection Pericope

Between the baptism and temptation narratives and the call of the first disciples, all of the Synoptic Gospels provide at least a glimpse of the one to whom those disciples responded. Matthew and Mark present only brief summaries of Jesus' message (Matt. 4:17//Mark 1:14b–15). Luke also begins with a summary statement (Luke 4:14–15), but it centers on Jesus himself and not on the content of his message. That summary is followed by accounts of five encounters of Jesus with various groups and individual persons prior to the call of the first disciples (Luke 5:1–11):

a. 4:16–30—the rejection at Nazareth
b. 4:31–37—teaching and exorcism in Capernaum
c. 4:38–39—the healing of Peter's mother-in-law
d. 4:40–41—summaries of healings and exorcisms
e. 4:42–44—Jesus resolves to take his message to other cities; summary of the content of his message

Events b through e are found in the same order in Mark immediately following the call of the first disciples. It might seem, therefore, that the Nazareth pericope (event a) is simply substituted for the summary of Jesus' message in Mark 1:14b–15.[3] If that is the case, the only substantive difference in Luke's account is the later presentation of the call of the disciples, which might be attributed to the apparently different source on which he drew for his account of that episode.

Further examination shows, however, that Mark's summary statement is not omitted by Luke, but is incorporated with Mark 1:38 into Luke 4:43. There Luke does not merely introduce the one whom the disciples follow, but also recapitulates what has already been said about Jesus' activity and significance. The healings and exorcisms, Jesus' teaching and preaching, his self-interpretation, and his interaction with hostile neighbors are all presented not just as things Jesus does, but as elaborations of who he is. That picture of Jesus is given shape and definition by the two parallel statements of the purpose for which Jesus has been sent, which introduce and close this section of the chapter (Luke 4:18–19 and 4:43), and which portray Jesus as the one who announces the good news of God's eschatological reign.

Jesus' Rejection at Nazareth

All three Synoptic Gospels contain an account of the hostile reception of Jesus by his neighbors in Nazareth. Both Mark and Matthew contain brief accounts and suggest that the episode occurred after Jesus' ministry was well under way (Mark 6:1–6a//Matt. 13:54–58). In Luke, however, the account of Jesus' rejection at Nazareth is presented in greater detail, and it is the core of Luke's inaugural portrait of Jesus. Questions about the literary relationship between the versions of the account, and consequently about the social context in which the Lukan account should be understood, can best be addressed following an analysis of the Lukan account itself. Since the focal point of the Lukan rejection pericope is the quotation from Isaiah, the analysis of the pericope must begin with the quotation itself, and with the way it is incorporated and interpreted in the narrative.

The Quotation from Isaiah.   The quotation from Isaiah is in fact a composite text. One phrase has been omitted from Isa. 61:1, and a phrase from Isa. 58:6 has been inserted. Furthermore, the language of the quotation is so close to that of the LXX that it appears to depend on it and not on an independent translation either from the Hebrew or from a Targum. In fact, the common word for "release" *(aphesis)* found in the LXX of Isa. 61:1 and 58:6, compared with the quite different wording in the two verses in the Hebrew text, suggests that the two verses may have been combined on the basis of the Greek text. That combination and the omission of the phrase from Isa. 61:1 are easy to understand if the text was being quoted from memory, as indeed was often the case at the time when the account took shape in the Greek text of the Gospel or in the pre-Gospel traditions in the Greek-speaking church. This would suggest that the quotation in its present form is indeed a product of the early church, which appears to have presented the text in the form in which the people were accustomed to hear the Scriptures.

The text not only is composite in form, but also has been noticeably abridged in that the last two phrases of Isa. 61:2 appear to have been omitted. Such selective reading of Scripture was not an accepted practice in Jesus' day, and in fact Joachim Jeremias suggests that if Jesus did read the text in such an abbreviated form that could have been a factor in provoking the anger of the townspeople.[4] What seems more likely is that the omission was the choice of whoever incorporated the quotation into its present narrative setting. In this context, the proclamation of the "acceptable year" *(eniautos dektos)* introduces a play on words resumed in the proverb in Luke 4:24.[5]

The Synagogue Service.   The narrative setting in which the quotation is found is a synagogue service in Nazareth. It is of course impossible to prove that this represents an event actually remembered from Jesus' lifetime. The most that might be determined is whether the event as described would be consistent with what is known about such services, or, on the other hand, whether it fits better the liturgical and hermeneutical practices of the early church. Unfortunately, what is known about the liturgical practices of the first-century synagogue and of the early church is quite limited, and the problem is further complicated by ambiguities within the story itself.

At the outset, we are told that Jesus was handed a *biblion*, which can mean either a "book" or a "scroll," and that he opened it to the text from Isaiah. If we assume for the moment that this is not a narrative composed by Luke or by the early church to summarize Jesus' agenda and to account for his experience of opposition, then the way the text from Isaiah came to be chosen is an important question. The question is basically whether we are to understand that Jesus was handed a text already selected either by the synagogue official or according to a prescribed lectionary reading, or that he selected the text on purpose to interpret his mission.

The lectionary hypothesis is suspect for several reasons. To begin with, it is doubtful that lectionaries including readings from the prophets were even in use in Jesus' day.[6] Second, the fact that the quotation may have been composite and seems clearly to have been abridged is contrary to the practice followed in any known synagogue lectionaries. Third, neither the notion of an established lectionary reading nor that of a text preselected by the synagogue official is either confirmed or denied by the situation described in Luke 4:17 itself. The ambiguity of that verse is centered in the word *biblion*, coupled with a text-critical problem surrounding the word "open," on which both internal and external evidence is moot.[7]

If the incident has any basis in Jesus' ministry, then, the means by which the text would have been preselected for him is at best unclear. It is at least possible that he would have selected the text himself. Indeed, as the following discussion will make clear, it seems that Jesus did make use of the images and language of Isa. 61:1–2 to interpret his ministry, so it would not be unlikely for the pre-Gospel tradition to refer to one or more occasions where he referred to the text itself.

We are told that following the reading of the text, Jesus sat down, as if he were about to begin to preach. Just where one would expect to find a sermon *interpreting* the text just presented, Luke records instead Jesus' words about the *fulfillment* of that scripture. In fact, the remainder of the pericope deals with the meaning of that fulfillment and the townspeople's response to it, rather than with the content of the verses from Isaiah.[8]

The Townspeople's Response.   The townspeople's initial reaction is depicted as one of amazement. The "words of grace" that Jesus spoke surely are intended to mean the message of God's promises and blessings recorded in Isaiah, and also the news that the promised time is present for Jesus' hearers. The suggestion that such promises might be fulfilled in their midst and at the word of one of their neighbors appears to be what prompts the response recorded in 4:22. Unlike the Markan version of this story (Mark 6:1–6a//Matt. 13:54–58), where the people's astonishment at Jesus' wisdom and works leads directly to their taking offense at him (Mark 6:3), the Lukan account begins with their being amazed and confused. The verbs *thaumazō* ("wonder" or "be amazed") and *martureō* ("bear witness"), which are peculiar to the Lukan account, do not have hostile connotations in the Lukan writings.[9] Furthermore, the Lukan form of the question about Jesus' relatives—"Is this not Joseph's son?"—does not carry the implied negative connotation of the Markan form where Jesus is referred to as "the son of Mary." It seems rather that Luke's form of the townspeople's question is ironic, and betrays what Luke considers to be the questioners' misunderstanding, for it is of course not as Joseph's son but as God's son that Jesus speaks the gracious words.[10]

From an initial response of amazement, the mood of the townspeople changes drastically by Luke 4:28, apparently in response to Jesus' further amplification of the meaning of his announcement in 4:21. The proverb in 4:23 marks an important step in that change of mood. Immediately prior to this verse, Jesus has been made aware of the amazement and confusion that his statement has evoked. By means of the proverb, he addresses in a colloquial fashion the attitudes and assumptions underlying that response: "Next thing I know you'll be saying to me, 'Charity begins at home. Don't forget your neighbors when all of this starts to happen.' "[11] Verse 24 then becomes the verse in which the bite of Jesus' message begins to be felt, for it stands as a blunt response to such assumptions on the part of his audience. This may not be a case where "charity begins at home" because what is at stake here is prophecy, and the prophet often must speak a hard and unpopular word to those closest at hand. The assumptions and amazement attributed to Jesus' neighbors are brought up short when those people encounter the work and message of a prophet, with whom the home town and its people cannot assume special privilege.[12]

In 4:25–27, Luke provides scriptural examples to account for the truth expressed in the proverb. The traditions referred to in those verses are 1 Kings 17 and 2 Kings 5. Those verses are usually understood to be an addition to the story by Luke, in order to suggest a connection between Jesus' rejection by and departure from the people of Nazareth, and the rejection of the gospel by the Jews and the subsequent Gentile mission.[13] It is possible, however, to account for these verses without recourse to an agenda of the early church that would have been foreign to Jesus' own day. In fact, these verses follow logically on 4:23–24 as part of a response from Jesus to the pretensions of his neighbors who claim a place of privilege at the time of fulfillment that Jesus had proclaimed. Since these verses invoke traditions in which Elijah and Elisha also carried out their prophetic witness outside the community of the chosen people, they would have underlined the point of those previous verses and could help to explain the eruption of the townspeople's wrath described in 4:28–29.

The graphic portrayal of the violence of their attack—attempting to run Jesus off a cliff—is without parallel in the NT. It might be understood as an escalation of the practice of casting a victim into a pit prior to stoning. If the people have concluded from Jesus' interpretation of his prophetic task in 4:24–27 that his appearance and proclamation are those of a false prophet, their response would be warranted by Torah (Deut. 13:1–5) and by precedent (Jer. 11:21–23). In any event, Jesus is said to have made his escape (4:30), and to have left his home town for good.

Event, Pre-Lukan Traditions, and Lukan Redaction. Considering the passage as it stands in Luke, however, leaves unresolved questions about the relationship among underlying event, pre-Lukan traditions, and Lukan redaction. These questions, in turn, are related to the social and ecclesiastical contexts in which the account must be interpreted, and to the impact that the collection of images found in it would have on those contexts. The direction generally followed in Lukan scholarship has been to interpret Luke's version of the story as his own composition based on Mark 6:1–6a and other details from non-Markan traditions. The core event from Mark would have contributed the location in a synagogue in Jesus' native region, the initial astonishment of the townspeople, a reference to Jesus' not doing any (or many) miracles in this region, the proverb about the unhappy fate of prophets in their home territory, and the neighbors' hostility to Jesus as the cause of his eventual departure from Nazareth. The three principal details added in the Lukan account are the content of the synagogue service, the references to the Elijah and Elisha traditions, and the violent ending.

The three details which have been added in Luke do not seem to be linked in any way that suggests that they formed a coherent narrative by themselves, or even that they reflect a single underlying source. The first two, however, refer to Hebrew Scriptures, and all three share the motif of prophecy. Together they change the Markan account considerably. First, they accentuate the theme of prophecy. Second, it is prophecy and not contempt brought on by over-familiarity or jealousy about miracles that provokes the people's hostility. Finally, these additions bring into the passage themes that are prominent in the remainder of Luke-Acts, such as the role of the Holy Spirit, the meaning of Jesus as "anointed one" and "prophet," "good news to the poor," "release" or "forgiveness," and the rejection of Jesus which would culminate in his passion and ultimate victory. The passage thereby becomes not only the inaugural event launching Jesus' ministry, but also a programmatic introduction of Jesus and a prefiguration of events to follow.[14]

Three factors challenge the apparent consensus that the Lukan rejection pericope is the result of Lukan redaction of an original Markan account. The first is the internal coherence and logic of the pericope as it stands, even as an event in Jesus' own lifetime, without having to import such Lukan concerns as the Gentile mission to account for such details as the Elijah and Elisha traditions represented in Luke 4:25–27. If the narrative as it stands is both coherent and understandable in a pre-Lukan historical setting, then it may be that the event itself was reported in a form similar to Luke's, which he then simply incorporated into his Gospel instead of the version found in Mark.

A second challenge to the former consensus is the linguistic evidence pointing to a non-Markan source for the Nazareth pericope which has been uncovered by H. Schürmann. He shows both that individual verses containing non-Markan traditions also contain non-Lukan (or pre-Lukan) words or ideas, and that these verses fit together in such a way as to indicate the presence of a complete narrative. Summarizing his findings concerning the redactional and tradition-historical issues in Luke 4:16–30, Schürmann attributes the form in Luke to Luke's minor polishing of a narrative of the Nazareth pericope found virtually complete in Q, immediately following the introductory statement also found in Q, which is represented in Luke 4:14–15. This independently developed variant of the tradition concerning the Nazareth incident would already have included the accents on prophecy that constitute the principal differences between the Lukan and Markan accounts.[15]

Finally, there is the challenge presented by the apparent difference between the internal and external hermeneutics by which the account is interpreted. It is clear that in the Lukan context, the church's concern for the spread of the gospel to the Gentiles is addressed in the dynamic of Jesus' own movement out of Nazareth under the shadow of the references to the Elijah and Elisha traditions. In the terminology coined by James Sanders, this would be a "constitutive" reading of the text. In a constitutive reading the blessings and promises of the gospel to which the text points are understood as belonging to an "in-group" (in this case, the church including the Gentile members), at the expense of an "out-group" (in this case, Jesus' neighbors and kinfolk, the Jews).[16]

In contrast to that constitutive reading is the "prophetic" hermeneutic implied in the story itself. In a prophetic reading the emphasis is on God's freedom to bless those whom God wills in the way that God wills. Thus, the townspeople of Nazareth are depicted as being provoked to rage at hearing the prophetic message which lets them know that they do not hold a place of privilege in the fulfillment of the promises of God depicted by the prophet Isaiah. Sanders suggests that, given the prominence of the motif of prophecy in the story itself, the prophetic hermeneutic may indeed have been part of the original incident in Jesus' own life. In addition to editorial work on the final form of the pericope, then, Luke's primary contribution would have been the reversing of that prophetic hermeneutic axiom in light of his perception of the situation of the church to which he wrote.[17]

It is of course impossible to prove or to disprove the historicity of the Nazareth episode as Luke portrays it, just as it is impossible to know for certain what may have been the pre-Gospel history of the account. If, however, there is at least the possibility that the account of the incident was formulated prior to its present occurrence in the Lukan context, it is important to ask how that account might have been received by its various audiences, as well as what the incident and the images by which it is developed may have meant in Jesus' own context.

If Sanders is correct, the Jubilee images found in the text from Isaiah were understood by Jesus' contemporaries as referring to blessings promised particularly to Israel at the time of God's eschatological reign. The prophetic reading of that text represented in the Nazareth pericope challenged that assumption of privilege, but left the socially revolutionary implications of the Jubilee imagery intact. In that way, the text of promise was turned into a threat: the poor to whom the good news would come and the captives who would be set free might be any of God's children. The bite of such a message would also have been felt in the early Palestinian church, if indeed the account found its way into the Gospel through the Q traditions that originated in that community. In the early Palestinian church, however, the bite of the message would have been lessened somewhat because of the relationship of that community to Jesus the Christ. On account of that relationship, the early church would have understood themselves to have the replaced Israel in having the primary claim to the fulfillment of the promises that Jesus announced.

Although Luke appears to have interpreted the account with a "constitutive" hermeneutic concerning the privileged position of the church in receiving the promised blessings, he has sustained and indeed developed the ethical implications of the Jubilee images themselves. Luke has done this by means of the remaining pericopes of chapter 4, which amplify the text from Isaiah into a picture of Jesus' identity and purpose that links Jesus to particular manifestations of physical and social change and summarizes his message as the proclamation of God's reign. In that way, Luke sets the stage for the interpretation of Jesus' life and ministry in the remainder of the Gospel in terms of the "good news to the poor" and "release" or "forgiveness" that mark humankind's encounter with the fact of God's sovereignty.

THE QUESTION FROM JOHN THE BAPTIST
(MATT. 11:2–6//LUKE 7:18–23)

The second place where Isa. 61:1–2 is cited directly is the account of the inquiry from John the Baptist concerning Jesus' identity. The account, drawn from Q, differs in only a few details in the two Gospels. John's question is whether Jesus is the "coming one," who is portrayed in Hebrew Scriptures as the prophet Elijah, the awaited Messiah, or God as initiator of the end time (Gen. 49:10; Ps. 118:26; Isa. 40:10; Daniel 7; Zech. 9:9; 14:5; Mal. 3:1–3). In all of the Synoptic Gospels, Mal. 3:1–3 is cited to describe John's work as forerunner (Mark 1:2; Matt. 11:10//Luke 7:27), and the one whom he awaits is painted as the "refiner" and "purifier" (Matt. 3:7–12//Mark 1:7–8//Luke 3:7–18).

At issue in the response to John's disciples is whether this "coming one" could be recognized by the activities outlined in the collage of texts from Isaiah (31:5–6; 29:18–19; 42:18; 43:8//6:10; 61:1–2), including the proclamation of good news to the poor and various sorts of healings, culminating in raising the dead. Two details of Jesus' identity are thus clarified and combined. First, the nature of the "coming one" as depicted by John is redefined. Second, when activities associated with the end time are linked to Jesus, the fulfillment of God's promises is so unexpected that it is a potential cause for scandal or stumbling (Matt. 11:6//Luke 7:23).

The parallels between this account and Luke's version of the rejection at Nazareth are clear. Not only are the citations from Isaiah similar, but so are the christological and hermeneutical points. Once again, the popular expectation of the nature of God's Anointed One (Christ/Messiah) is confronted. In Luke 4, the people express surprise that one of their neighbors should be so audacious as to claim to bring the fulfillment of the promises in Isa. 61:1–2. In the response to John's disciples, John's own anticipation of an apocalyptic figure (Matt. 3:11–12//Luke 3:16–18) is confronted. Just as the townspeople of Nazareth are offended at the "prophetic" conclusion that they would have no place of privilege at the time of fulfillment, so here the evidence of healing and of the proclamation of "good news to the poor" is portrayed as likely to provoke not celebration but "scandal." Those who would be scandalized would not be the people who had enjoyed those blessings of Jesus' ministry, but instead those who had taken offense at such acts.[18] On the other hand, those who would have recognized Jesus would have been precisely the "poor" and those caught in the pain of physical illness or social ostracism until they experienced the healing, freedom, and acceptance that came to them in Jesus' presence.

The Pre-Gospel History of the Account

The question of the historicity of this episode is a difficult one to resolve. Earlier in their Gospels, both Matthew and Luke have portrayed John as being privy to the nature of Jesus' mission, so the doubt implied in John's question runs counter to the agenda of both evangelists. Furthermore, one might expect that if the early church had invented the story there would have been at least some affirmation of Jesus attributed to John, especially since the story is followed by an account of Jesus' acclamation of John (Matt. 11:7–19//Luke 7:24–35). The response to the question from John that is attributed to Jesus is not an unequivocal one either, as one might have anticipated had the story been invented by the early church. Instead, Jesus appears to answer a question about his identity by reference to things taking place, without drawing an explicit connection between these events and himself. The story thus merely suggests what the early church would have wanted to proclaim plainly about Jesus' identity. Prompted by such questions and observations as these, one must recognize at least the possibility that the account is based on the reminiscence of an event from Jesus' life.

Whether or not that is the case, however, the account as it now stands in both Gospels is directed to the church. In both accounts

Jesus is introduced with christological titles—*christos* in Matthew and *kyrios* in Luke. Those titles make it clear that both versions of the account are directed to people who already recognize in the references from Isaiah ample evidence and confirmation of Jesus' identity. Those people would recognize themselves as the ones who are blessed because they "find no offense" in Jesus.

The Gospel Contexts

Furthermore, both evangelists use the contexts in which they set this pericope to accentuate its christological significance. In Matthew, the question from John introduces a new section of the Gospel following the commissioning and instruction of the Twelve. That section deals with people's recognition of and response to Jesus (Matt. 11:20–30). Sabbath controversies (Matt. 12:1–21) and the Beelzebub controversy (12:22–32) then reformulate the issue of the recognition of Jesus into the issue of the source of the power at work in Jesus.

The context of the inquiry from John in Luke resembles at several points the context of the quotation from Isaiah 61 in Luke 4. In both cases, the reference from Isaiah interprets the purpose and significance of Jesus in response to questions about whether Jesus could be the awaited one (Luke 4:22; 7:19–20). Again in both cases, the reaction (4:28–29) or anticipated reaction (7:23) is one of scandal or outright hostility. Linked to the reference from Isaiah are examples of Jesus' participation in the events that it outlines (4:31–44; 7:1–17, 21). Like Luke 4:16–44, Luke 7 appears to constitute a discrete section of the Gospel, sandwiched between the long Sermon on the Plain in Luke 6 and the collection of parables in Luke 8. The stories of the healing of the centurion's servant and of the raising of the widow's son at Nain (7:1–10, 11–17) provide evidence of Jesus' involvement in the activities referred to in the passages from Isaiah. These incidents also echo, in reverse order, the references to the Elijah and Elisha traditions in Luke 4:25–27. The one major theme of Isa. 61:1–2 that is not included in the collection of Isaianic material in Luke 7:22 is the theme of "release" or "forgiveness." That theme, however, is central to the story of the woman with the ointment (Luke 7:36–50), which is found immediately following Jesus' tribute to John (7:24–35) and which concludes this section of the Gospel and provides a thematic link to the summary statement about the women who accompany Jesus (8:1–3).

It is impossible to know whether Luke deliberately presented the material in chapter 7 to echo 4:16–44, but the way sources appear to have been interwoven suggests that the similarity is not coincidental. In chapter 4, Luke combines the account of the Nazareth pericope, which is either drawn from Q or compiled from several sources, with Markan material (4:31–44) to form a portrait by which Jesus is introduced to the readers prior to the call of the first disciples. In chapter 7, Luke again draws on Q, including a reference to Isa. 61:1–2 and other Isaianic material, and interweaves it with material from his special source, "L" (Luke 7:11–17, 36–50), as a summary of the early part of Jesus' ministry.

The resulting portraits of Jesus are strikingly similar. In both cases, Jesus is defined by passages from Isaiah, including the Jubilee text of Isa. 61:1–2. Whereas in chapter 4 that reference introduces the portrait, in chapter 7 it is found almost exactly at the center. In both accounts, the quotation or paraphrase is the organizing rubric for the surrounding pericopes that point to Jesus' power to heal, cast out demons, and otherwise mediate the transformative events outlined in the Isaianic passages. In both cases, Luke depicts Jesus as making that power known especially to people outside the community with which the covenant promises were generally associated. As a result, responses to Jesus vary from group to group and from person to person. At issue is the acceptability (chapter 4) and the recognition (chapter 7) of Jesus as the one in whom people meet the inaugural celebration of God's reign.

CONCLUSION

The images which coalesce around both of these references to Isaiah 61—"release" or "forgiveness" from that which enslaves, "good news to the poor," and the advent of God's reign in Jesus of Nazareth—must now be explored in the rest of the gospel traditions. The particular stories, parables, sayings, and other forms in which these images are presented will help to fill out the summary portraits in the Nazareth account and the response to John the Baptist, and to clarify the particular sense in which Jesus of Nazareth is the "one anointed" by the Spirit of God. As has been the case with the passages examined in this chapter, in those other passages also, the images drawn from the Jubilee traditions will be seen to have a different impact in the Gospel and pre-Gospel settings. These differences, and the social and ecclesiastical contexts that prompted them, will provide clues for our own hearing of the texts and for our reflection on the one whom the images portray.

CHAPTER 4

Jubilee Images
Elaborated

Proclaiming Good News
to the Poor

The phrase "proclaim good news to the poor" is found in its entirety in the Synoptic Gospels only in the quotations of Isa. 61:1–2, namely, in Luke 4:18–19 and Matt. 11:6//Luke 7:23. The two components of the phrase, however—"the proclamation of good news" and "the poor"—are much more common. In fact, the former is virtually synonymous with the early church's message about Jesus' life and teachings and about his work of salvation. In Hebrew Scriptures, "proclaiming good news" can refer to any message that conveys tidings of benefit to the recipient. The contexts in which the verb *bśr* is found, however, refer most often to God's saving acts and presence among humankind. The use of the Greek verb *euaggelizomai* and the related noun *euaggelion* as technical terms both for the content of Jesus' message and for the early church's message about Jesus is consistent with that meaning, in that the church recognized in Jesus the Christ God's ultimate act of salvation.[1]

The fact that these technical terms for the early church's confession about Jesus are central to the Jubilee traditions of Hebrew Scriptures, and particularly to Isa. 61:1–2, has two consequences for this study. First, in a negative sense, because *euaggelizomai* and *euaggelion* have become technical terms for the gospel message as a whole, it would not be appropriate to claim that every occurrence of one of these terms is evidence of a specific reference to Jubilee traditions. On the positive side, however, the fact that these terms have become synonymous with "the gospel" is added evidence of the importance of those traditions in defining Jesus' ministry.

"The poor" *(hoi ptōchoi)* are mentioned in several contexts in the Synoptic Gospels. Those contexts underline the importance of "the poor" in Jesus' ministry and in his identity as the Christ. They also expand the meaning of "the poor" to include people who are socially outcast or physically disabled, as well as people who are economically disadvantaged. Among these "poor," then, God's saving activity is being manifested. The Beatitudes found in both Matthew's and Luke's great sermons (Matt. 5:3–6//Luke 6:20–22) and the teachings on banquet etiquette found in Luke 14 are the principal places where "the poor" are listed with other groups as recipients of the blessing of God's eschatological reign. These lists parallel the one in Isa. 61:1–2, and they make explicit the ways in which the "liberty" of the Jubilee proclaimed by Jesus would be experienced. A second group of passages underlines the importance of "the poor" by linking one's response to the poor with one's relationship to Jesus and to the reign of God which he proclaims. It is to these two groups of passages that we will now turn.

RECOGNIZING "THE POOR"

The Beatitudes (Matt. 5:3–6//Luke 6:20–22)

The Sermon on the Mount in Matthew and the Sermon on the Plain in Luke begin with a common core of blessings, which both Gospel writers have expanded and presented in slightly different form.

The blessings common to both Gospels are:

Matthew	Luke
1. v. 3—the poor in spirit	v. 20b—you poor
2. v. 4—those who mourn	v. 21b—you who weep
3. v. 6—those who hunger and thirst for righteousness	v. 21a—you who hunger
4. vv. 11–12—you when they revile you	vv. 22–23—you when people hate you

Matthew's blessings are combined with five others, all in the third person. In Luke the four blessings are joined to four woes (all in the second person) against people in circumstances opposite to those in the benedictions. Both the woes and Luke's version of the blessings are in the second person. Arguments in favor of either of the forms of the Beatitudes being closer to an original which the other Gospel writer then changed are inconclusive.

Differences in the second and fourth of the common beatitudes are largely stylistic rather than substantive. Matthew's second beatitude echoes the wording of Isa. 61:2b ("to comfort all who mourn"), whereas Luke describes more concretely the same reversal of circumstances. The fourth beatitude in both Gospels contrasts persecution suffered now with blessings to come. Differences in language in the remaining two, however, require closer examination.

Most scholars agree that Matthew's version of the first beatitude is an elaboration of an original which said simply, "Blessed are the poor." The question at issue is whether the two forms of the beatitude differ in meaning. Does one refer simply to an economic condition while the other refers to an attitude parallel to that of "the meek" in Matt. 5:5? D. Flusser has argued that the wording in Matt. 5:3 and 5 represents a combination of "the poor" from Isa. 61:1–2, "the humble and contrite in spirit" from Isa. 66:2, and "the meek" from Ps. 37:11. Flusser notes that this combination of texts is also characteristic of the Qumran literature (1QH xviii 14–15; 1QM xiv 3, 7; 1QS iii 8; iv 3). He suggests, therefore, that Matthew's first three beatitudes originated either at Qumran or in some milieu close to the Qumran sect.[2] What the Qumran evidence makes clear, however, is not necessarily a literary or historical connection between that community and Matthew's form of the Beatitudes, but rather a nuance of Hebrew words for "the poor" which would have been understood in Jesus' context or in the early Palestinian church.

Flusser's argument rests on the need for ʿānî ("humble") in Isa. 66:2 to be combined with ʿănāwîm ("poor") in Isa. 61:1 in order for the latter to mean "poor in spirit." In fact, however, the two terms are similar in meaning, and both are translated in the LXX by ptōchos ("poor") and by praüs ("humble" or "meek"). Anyone familiar with that background could easily interpret the dative of respect ("in spirit") as being implied in Isa. 61:1. In that case, it is clear that Matthew's first beatitude does not differ in meaning from Luke's, but rather captures a nuance of the meaning of "the poor" present in Hebrew Scriptures but not part of the Greek work ptōchos. In both cases, the accent is on the blessing as part of the liberation from pain and oppression that marks God's eschatological reign. In neither case should the blessing be seen as a reward either for particular moral behavior or attitudes, as Matthew's version has often been understood, or for some qualification inherent in the condition of economic poverty, as Luke's version might seem to suggest.

In the third of the common beatitudes it appears that Matthew has again elaborated a simpler blessing in a way that accents a meaning implied in the simpler form. The word "righteousness" *(dikaiosynē)* is a characteristically Matthean word. It occurs only once in the Synoptic Gospels outside of Matthew (Luke 1:75) and seven times in Matthew, of which five are in the Sermon on the Mount (Matt. 3:15; 5:6, 10, 20; 6:1, 33; 21:32). Two of those occurrences (5:20 and 6:1) seem clearly to refer to a quality of human behavior. Of the others, 3:15; 6:33; and 21:32 all refer to God's saving activity and sovereign will. Since in 5:10 people persecuted for "righteousness" are promised "the realm of heaven," the cause of persecution should probably be understood as "longing for God's saving activity," and not "desiring good behavior" or even "desiring justice" as an ethical value. Furthermore, that beatitude is followed immediately by the one speaking of persecution "for my sake," which makes Jesus himself parallel to "righteousness" in the previous blessing. In that larger context, then, Matt. 5:6—"Blessed are those who hunger and thirst for righteousness"—should also be understood as a blessing and promise of satisfaction for those yearning for God's saving activity.

The intimate connection between that yearning and physical hunger is clear in Hebrew Scriptures. Among a people who lived with the constant threat of famine and scarcity of water, the experience of hunger and thirst was a paradigm of the experience of God's judgment or silence (Isa. 29:8; Lam. 4:4, 9; Job 24:10–11; Deut. 28:47–48), and the satisfaction of hunger was seen as one of the signs of God's presence and advocacy (Isa. 32:6; 49:7–10; 65:13; Pss. 107:4–9, 35–36; 146:5–10; Neh. 9:15). Thus the two versions of the blessing are indeed parallel in meaning for both recognize that the basic human need for food is paradigmatic of all the needs that are met in the establishment of God's reign.

These four beatitudes recapitulate the themes of Isa. 61:1–2, but present them in the form of a graphic contrast between present suffering and the blessings that are at hand. In occupied Palestine of Jesus' day, as well as in the early church both there and in the Diaspora, many people knew firsthand the pain of hunger, poverty, grief, and persecution. Such an accent on the reversal of circumstances would reach into the midst of people's pain to make vivid and concrete the promises to which the ancient witnesses pointed.

At the same time, even in the situation of the occupation there were those who suffered less. Some learned to profit economically or socially from the occupation. For others, such as the religious leaders, position and office may have provided relative prestige and comfort despite the larger social and political context. To such relatively privileged people, the Beatitudes doubtless brought more threat than comfort. Those people need not have been immoral or to have acquired their profits or positions dishonestly. In some sense, however, the old order was working for them. That basis for their security would have been so fragile and tenuous that any word about a reversal of values or about the establishment of a new reign would represent a threat to their situation. Such a new order might be called "the reign of God," but people clinging to their status in the present order would hesitate to associate themselves with it, for they would see themselves as having something to lose. Then as now, the unknown represents a risk for those with a stake in the old order. For "the poor" it could only mean a promise.

Banquet Etiquette (Luke 14:12–24)

A collection of teachings and a parable centered around a great feast develop even more graphically the meaning of "the poor" who encounter God's reign in Jesus of Nazareth and the reversal of values that God's reign entails. Luke sets the teachings and parable in the context of a Sabbath meal at the home of a Pharisee, a context that itself carries the ambivalent qualities of a festive event at a holy time, but in a place where hearers of the gospel would have come to expect opposition to Jesus and confrontation of him by religious leaders. The ambivalence of the setting is sustained in the teachings and parable themselves, where the festivity, the confrontation, and the locus of holiness shift to new positions in the face of a prophetic interpretation of God's promises.

The events occurring at the supper form a self-contained unit with no direct connections to the immediate literary context. The Sabbath setting and the presence of "lawyers and Pharisees" are essential to the controversy associated with the healing of the man with edema (Luke 14:1–6). That particular story is found only in Luke, and appears to come from his special source (L), but it is similar to the

Markan account of the healing of the man with the withered hand (Matt. 12:9–14//Mark 3:1–6//Luke 6:6–11) and to the Lukan story of the bent-over woman (Luke 13:10–17).

The Teachings. The teachings that follow (Luke 14:7–15) develop the imagery associated with a meal and with the entertainment of guests, but they do not refer to the Sabbath. These teachings are also unique to Luke, except for the saying in Luke 14:11, which has parallels in Matt. 18:4; 23:12; and Luke 18:14. The teachings may have been found already joined to the story in Luke 14:1–6, since they also portray a proper event interrupted by something unexpected. Because the story deals with Torah observance and the teachings with social custom, however, the connection is not that close, and Luke may have combined them at the same time that he provided the setting including both the Sabbath and the banquet themes.

The teachings themselves may have been combined by Luke or by his source on the basis of the reference to a meal. The teachings can be divided into two clusters according to both their content and the change of address from the guests (14:7) to the host (14:12). Without the saying in 14:11, the teachings in 14:7–10 sound like folk wisdom advising prudence in social settings. The reversal of first and last is a consequence of misjudgment about one's own status relative to the other guests, and not the matter of principle that 14:11 would suggest. That verse seems to be an artificial attempt to bring the previous teaching into line with the reversal of values depicted in 14:12–14 and the subsequent parable.

If 14:7–11 seems to be a page from a first-century book of etiquette, complete with warnings of the embarrassing consequences of missing one's social cue, 14:12–14 is far from a counsel of common sense. Instead, these verses call for the inversion of the usual reasons for inviting guests:[3] none of those to be invited would be able to return an invitation, and they are the sort of people whose presence would be most apt to make more typical guests uncomfortable. In addition to depicting that startling reversal of values, the teaching ends by attributing eternal consequences to one's table community (14:14b). These consequences are then elaborated in a beatitude pointing to the messianic banquet (14:15), which provides both a transition to the parable (14:16–24) and the key to recognizing the teaching and the parable as referring to the reign of God.

The Parable.   The parable develops in much greater detail the picture of a banquet at which the guest list and rules of etiquette have been changed. A comparison of the versions of the parable found in Luke 14:16–24, Matt. 22:1–10, and *Gos. Thom.* 64 suggests that the original parable had four parts: the giving of a feast or banquet, the reissuing of earlier invitations, the making of excuses by the people who had been invited, and the issuing of a new set of invitations so that the banquet could take place. Each version of the parable has acquired particular accents that have resulted in three different stories, of which only Luke's develops the theme of the identity and fate of the poor.[4]

The excuses of the first guests and the identity of their replacements are the two points in the story where Luke develops his particular interpretation. On the story level, the excuses appear specious and contrived and somewhat inconsistent. The first two (14:18–19) seem to anticipate tardiness rather than absence, with the expectation of arriving after the banquet was under way but prior to the end of the first course, as custom allowed. The reasons given appear to be a blend of sloppy commercial practices and a certain disregard for the host of the banquet. The third excuse (14:20) seems to anticipate absence from the banquet, as well as being the result of total absentmindedness!

Despite the contrary indication in Luke 14:20, it would have been most consistent with ancient banquet etiquette to understand the excuses as reasons for the guests' late arrival, after their daily business was finished. In Luke's version of the parable, however, the banquet to which they have been invited operates by a different set of rules. At this banquet, delays for business as usual are not permitted, and latecomers find their places taken by a new cast of celebrants.

The real nature of this banquet is made clear by two devices. First, there is the internal device of the ambiguity of Luke 14:24. In this verse we suddenly find the plural of the second person pronoun, when up to that point one servant has been addressed. To dismiss the verse as simply part of the setting—a comment attributed to Jesus concerning participation in the messianic banquet—belies the way it remains linked to the parable itself. The verse appears instead to be a transparent overlay on which the lines of the parable's outline are drawn, but through which Luke's intended point of reference can be glimpsed: the feast from which the reluctant and self-preoccupied guests have excluded themselves is the feast of God's realm.

In addition to that internal device, there is an external one, namely, the echoes of these excuses in Hebrew Scriptures. They are remarkably similar to the first three of the four reasons for deferment from the army in the Holy War of God (Deut. 20:5–8). Those four excuses are: having built a house but not yet dedicated it; having planted a vineyard the fruit of which one has not yet enjoyed; having married but not yet consummated the marriage; and being fainthearted. In the parable, however, the host does not consider the excuses adequate grounds for deferring participation in the banquet. Whether Luke intended to call to mind this list from Deuteronomy is of course impossible to know. Given the importance of both the messianic banquet and the holy war as images related to Jewish eschatological expectation, such a reference would not be impossible, particularly at a pre-Lukan stage of the tradition. If such a reference is present, it makes the point of how the reign of God transcends traditional expectation and confounds those who might have thought themselves to be protected from the need for an immediate response to such a moment.

Already the excuses of the first group have provided clues both to the character of this reign of which the parable speaks, and to social customs and religious laws that no longer serve to protect one from the demands or the unmerited joy which that reign offers. One can imagine the growing uneasiness of any hearers who might have been counting on just such protection! In Luke's version of the parable, however, our attention is drawn not only to the excluded guests, but also to the identity of their replacements who will enjoy the feast.

Luke describes two expeditions to find guests to replace those who have declined the first invitation. The second of these expeditions, in which no details are given about the people to be brought, resembles the single expedition described in Matthew and the *Gospel of Thomas*. It is the account of the first expedition that bears the hallmark of Luke's editorial work, for the categories of invitees echo lists found elsewhere in his Gospel of those groups of people to whom the message of "good news" is particularly directed.[5]

The list of those whom the servant is to find—the poor and those who are maimed, blind, and lame—is identical to the list of those to be invited to one's banquet according to the teaching in Luke 14:13. What is even more striking is the similarity between those lists and the groups of people singled out to receive the blessings of God's reign according to the Beatitudes and in the Jubilee text of Isaiah:

Luke 4:18	*Matt. 11:5//Luke 7:22*
poor	blind
captives	lame
blind	lepers
oppressed	deaf
	dead
	poor

Matt. 5:3, 4, 5, 6, 11//Luke 6:20–22

poor	poor
mourners	hungry
hungry	mourners
persecuted	persecuted

Luke 14:13 and 21

poor	poor
maimed	maimed
lame	blind
blind	lame

In those lists once again, God's reign—here symbolized in the great feast where hunger and sadness are replaced by plenty and rejoicing—has been interpreted as encompassing those people usually denied access to human occasions of celebration, as well as to the benefits of the social, political, and economic order. The poor, the suffering, and the oppressed become participants in the promises of God's reign, and the promises themselves accent precisely the points at which people's present circumstances bring them pain.

This reversal of values and circumstances is accentuated when one compares these lists with others in the literature of Second Temple Judaism and in Hebrew Scriptures that deal with people excluded from special roles in the religious life of the community. Those excluded from the Aaronic priesthood (Lev. 21:17–23), those denied membership in the Qumran community (1QSa ii 5–22), and those not allowed to take part in the holy war (1QM vii 4–6)[6] include all the categories found in the Gospel lists noted above except "the poor." That difference is significant, for in both Hebrew Scriptures and the literature of Qumran, "the poor" is frequently used as a designation for Israel, and especially for the elect within Israel. In the Gospel lists, this term of favor is joined to categories of those who are outcast. In their association with "the poor," their former exclusion is canceled in a celebration of divine hospitality at the banquet of God's reign. At the same time, by being joined to other categories of people whose literal physical condition is at issue, the term "the poor" retains its literal reference to those who are economically impoverished and cannot be reduced to a religious or spiritual category.

Within Luke's parable, the guest list functions as a commentary on the theme of election. That theme is introduced in the verbs *kaleō* and *parakaleō* which are found with the meaning of "invite" or "call" only in Luke 14, 15, and 16. The presence of these words in material drawn from different sources[7] suggests that Luke may have introduced the theme of election in this section of the Gospel. Indeed, all of the occurrences of these words seem to contradict the notion that suffering is an indication of God's disfavor, which is a common distortion of the Deuteronomic principle that obedience brings blessing. Those who support that distortion would identify with the first guests, and Luke challenges such people from two directions. In the teaching section, it is their life style or value structure that is called into question. When the invitation to the banquet is issued and they turn out to have excluded themselves from the feast by presuming on their chosenness, it is their very identity that is challenged.

Even if those in the community to which Luke wrote understood themselves as the heirs of the outcasts to whom Jesus' message was brought, and consequently read chapter 14 as a new basis on which to assume their election, the bite of the original teaching and parable is still felt. Such presumption is always overturned in the drama of the parable itself, for as soon as such an assumption is made, the guest list is changed: "the poor" are always those who have nothing on which to presume.

"The poor" in the Gospel are thus all those people without presumption of privilege, to whom Jesus' message comes as good news. There are very few to whom that message is totally good news, because most people claim something that sets them over others—

age, or gender, or race, or religion, or ability, or health—even if they are economically poor. Therefore, an understanding of "the poor" as an economic category (which it always remains), but also as a category of people that includes those whom the tradition labels as outcasts, enables us to avoid idealizing the economic condition of poverty. The point of these Gospel texts is that the word about God's sovereignty *is* a word of promise particularly for those who can find no security or hope in the structures of human institutions or the plans of human rulers. To those "poor" the news of God's reign *is* a welcome message. To them the invitation goes out to begin the feast and to share in the banquet.

RESPONDING TO THE POOR

In addition to redefining "the poor" to whom the message of God's reign comes as good news, the Gospels also draw connections between people's response to the poor and their relationship to Jesus as the Christ and to the reign that he announced. Three accounts will be examined under this rubric: the stories of the rich young man, of Zacchaeus the chief tax collector, and of the woman at Bethany.

The Rich Young Man
(Mark 10:17–22//Matt. 19:16–22//Luke 18:18–23)

The versions of the story in Matthew and Luke differ only in minor details from the original in Mark. This pronouncement story, built around the saying in Mark 10:21, begins with a question from an onlooker about the means to gain eternal life (Mark 10:17). The questioner is directed to the commandments found in the Torah, which he claims to observe already (Mark 10:19–20). Finally, in the climax of the incident Jesus tells him, by means of the saying in Mark 10:21, the one thing lacking to assure his goal: "Go, sell what you have, and give to the poor . . . and come, follow me."[8]

The story itself and the sayings in Mark 10:13–16 and 10:23–31, to which the story was joined either by Mark or in the pre-Markan tradition, develop such themes as wealth, the reign of God, and eternal life. The final clause of the story, "come, follow me," introduces the theme of following Jesus, which otherwise does not occur until Mark 10:28. In 10:28 the specific sacrifices made by Peter and the others are mentioned, and their fate is contrasted with that of the rich man. The theme of following Jesus is developed further in the Markan context through the account of Jesus' third passion prediction (Mark 10:32–34) and the dispute between James and John about greatness (Mark 10:35–45). These constitute a final set of teachings on that theme prior to the passion account, and indeed occur after the final stage of Jesus' journey to Jerusalem was already under way.

Without the reference to following Jesus, the saying in Mark 10:21 would be like a proverb or wisdom saying about the blessings that come to those who are generous and charitable. The man's response would be a reaction to the difficulty of parting with one's possessions. The sayings on the incompatibility of wealth and the realm of God (10:23–24) are related in subject matter to this simple version of the story. They appear, however, to be an intrusion into the story as it now stands, for 10:28 deals not with a reward for charity or with the dangers of wealth, but with what it means to follow Jesus. Peter is said to contrast himself and the others who have left everything and followed Jesus with the rich man who is not able to do so. The saying in 10:21 and what is said of the disciples in 10:29–30 are not exactly parallel, however, either in structure or in content. Furthermore, the description of the rewards or consequences in 10:30 contains much greater detail than does the description of the disappointment of the rich man in 10:22. Nevertheless, Mark 10:21 and 10:29–30 have the following common elements:

1. That which is given up (vv. 21 and 29);
2. A relationship to Jesus (v. 21: following Jesus; v. 29: for Jesus' sake);
3. Additional motivation (v. 21: "give to the poor"; v. 29: "for the gospel");
4. Promised rewards (v. 21: "treasure in heaven" [v. 17 also implies eternal life]; v. 30: to "receive a hundredfold now . . . and in the age to come eternal life").

What this comparison of Mark 10:21 with 10:29–30 makes clear is that in 10:21 "the poor" are not simply those to whom charity is to be shown. Instead, the gift to the poor is portrayed as virtually equivalent to the cause of the gospel, which, together with following Jesus himself, is the basis of discipleship.

Zacchaeus (Luke 19:1–10)

Another person whose promised gift to the poor is interpreted as more than a pledge of charity is the chief tax collector Zacchaeus.

The story of Zacchaeus, found only in Luke, is set near the end of Jesus' journey to Jerusalem. It is separated from the story of the rich man by only a passion prediction (Luke 18:31–34) and the account of the healing of a blind man at Jericho (18:35–43). The reference to "the poor" in the story is in Zacchaeus's puzzling promise to distribute half of his possessions to them.

The story of Zacchaeus has many details in common with the story of the call of a lesser tax official named Levi, with which Luke begins the account of Jesus' ministry in Galilee (Luke 5:27–32//Matt. 9:9–13//Mark 2:14–17). In fact, the two stories about tax collectors may indeed go back to a common tradition.[9] There is, however, an important difference. In the story of Levi, Jesus is portrayed as responding immediately to the objections raised by onlookers concerning his association with such a person.[10] In the story of Zacchaeus, on the other hand, the response of Jesus is separated from the complaint by the promise in Luke 19:8.

That verse presents several problems. First, it begins by announcing that Zacchaeus spoke *pros ton kyrion*. It is unclear whether the intent is to depict Zacchaeus in an attitude of prayer (addressing God), or whether *kyrios* is a confessional title ascribed to Jesus by the early church or by Luke in the retelling of the story. If the latter is the case, it is evidence for the late addition of this verse to a narrative which otherwise calls Jesus by name.[11] Second, the intent of the promise in 19:8 is obscure,[12] as is its relationship to the declaration in 19:9–10 in which that promise is not mentioned as grounds for Zacchaeus's restoration to full membership in the house of Israel.

A clue to the interpretation of 19:8 can be found in a comparison of that response to Jesus by Zacchaeus with the response attributed to Levi (Luke 5:28//Matt. 9:9//Mark 2:14). On the one hand, Levi is said to have followed Jesus. On the other hand, the consequences for Zacchaeus are found in his promise in 19:8, which contains the reference to providing for "the poor." Both responses are presented in a favorable light as appropriate results of the encounters with Jesus. It would appear, therefore, that once again following Jesus is portrayed as parallel to generous behavior toward "the poor."

Although the specific language of "proclaiming good news" and "release" is not found in Luke 19:1–10, the story exemplifies both these aspects of Jesus' ministry. Zacchaeus's attention to the needs of the poor is prompted by or at least related to his own experience of

Jesus' crossing of the boundaries set by society, and of his setting Zacchaeus free from the exclusion imposed upon him because of his profession. Zacchaeus's response is "discipleship," in which the message encountered in Jesus' presence is carried forward by one not formally named among Jesus' followers. Luke has told this story of Zacchaeus just before the passion narrative, when the possibility of following Jesus on his earthly mission would be superseded by the church's vocation of faithfulness to the risen Christ. In the Lukan context, therefore, this story functions as a summons to the church to recognize the consequences for its own behavior of the redemption it has encountered in Jesus—behavior in which concern for the poor is an appropriate vehicle for confessing Jesus as the Christ.[13]

The Woman at Bethany
(Matt. 26:6–13//Mark 14:3–9)

One's response to "the poor" is also associated with the confession of Jesus as the Christ in the story of the anointing at Bethany.[14] The story is presented in virtually identical form in Matthew and Mark. Its principal points are:

1. The woman's extravagance in anointing Jesus' head[15] (Matt. 26:7//Mark 14:3);
2. The objection to the waste of the ointment instead of its sale to provide for the poor (Matt. 26:8–9//Mark 14:4–5);
3. Jesus' words of commendation to the woman and his statement about the poor (Matt. 26:10–12//Mark 14:6–8);
4. Jesus' assurance that the woman's deed would be remembered wherever the gospel is preached (Matt. 26:13//Mark 14:9).

If one takes the story out of context, it appears to contradict the message of "good news to the poor," for in this account Jesus is said to rebuke those who are concerned about the poor and to praise the woman's apparent extravagance. To draw such a conclusion, however, would be to deny the significance of the place in the Gospel narrative in which this account is found, and also to fail to pay close attention to the saying about "the poor." The anointing story in Matthew and Mark (like the similar story in John 12:1–8) is set in the midst of the passion narrative, at a point when Jesus' approaching death is coming into sharper focus. This story is set between the account of the conspiracy against Jesus by the religious establishment and that of Judas's plan to betray Jesus. In that context, the words attributed to

Jesus concerning the woman's act compliment its timeliness and its appropriateness without denying the importance of the others' concern for the poor.

The saying about the poor substantiates the conclusion that, far from denying the significance of care for the poor, this episode interprets that concern against the background of the extraordinary demands of the impending crisis in Jesus' life. In fact, the parallelism of the clauses of Mark 14:7–8a (RSV) essentially equates the woman's act at that moment with a continuing commitment to care for the poor:

a.   ongoing time: "For you always have the poor with you" (v. 7a);
b.   appropriate action: "Whenever you will, you can do good to them" (v. 7b);
a′.   immediate crisis: "But you will not always have me" (v. 7c);
b′.   appropriate action: "She has done what she could" (v. 8a).

The difference between the two actions (b and b′) is not the superiority of one over the other, but rather the difference between an ongoing need (a) and the urgency of a one-time event (a′). Mark, or the community to which this formulation of the story and interpretation of the anointing of Jesus is to be attributed, thus appears to be saying that the question of discipleship, or of one's relationship to Jesus and the gospel, is intimately related to one's relationship to and care for the poor.

The story of the anointing at Bethany once again makes it clear that to proclaim the gospel, both as Jesus' message and as the story of his life and ministry, is first of all to proclaim "good news to the poor." It is a short step from this story to the perspective of the parable of the Great Judgment (Matt. 25:31–49), where the enthroned and sovereign Christ is explicitly identified with the hungry, the thirsty, the stranger, the naked, the sick, and the imprisoned, and where one's case before the heavenly tribunal is resolved on the basis of one's responsiveness to the human faces of Christ in the poor and oppressed.

CHAPTER 5

Jubilee Images
Elaborated

"Release" or "Forgiveness"

The proclamation of "release" or "forgiveness" in Jubilee traditions of Hebrew Scriptures refers both to the release of slaves and the cancellation of debts (Leviticus 25), and to the liberty proclaimed to captives and other prisoners (Isa. 58:6; 61:1–2). In the LXX the verb *aphiēmi* and the related noun *aphesis* are used to express this aspect of the Jubilee proclamation. Such usage is consistent with the secular, legal significance that these words had in classical Greek where they referred to one's release from bonds, debts, or other legal requirements.

These same words are also used in the LXX, however, to translate verbs of remission, of which sin or guilt is the object and God the subject. Such a usage not only represents the occurrence in a religious context of a term originally associated with the secular sphere, but also "significantly modifies the verbs of remission or forgiveness, since the original sense of the Hebrew verbs is that of cultic removal and expiation of sin, while *aphienai* has a legal sense."[1] The effect of the use of this verb in the LXX is thus felt in two directions. First, the Greek word itself takes on the meaning of forgiveness in a religious or ethical sense. Second, the vocabulary for forgiveness in Hebrew Scriptures is broadened beyond the primarily cultic terminology of cleansing or purification into a more contractual or covenantal emphasis.

In the NT the verb *aphiēmi* is found with monetary debts (Matt. 18:27, 32), "captives" (Luke 4:18), and "sin" (Matt. 6:14–15; Mark

2:5–10; 3:28; Luke 7:47–50) as its objects.[2] Indeed, ethical and cultic concerns in general can be distinguished but not separated in Gospel usage. Both are means of talking about the effect of the advent of God's reign in breaking the tyranny of evil in all of its forms. In that context, "release" is more than a metaphor for God's work of redemption and reconciliation, and the economic image of the cancellation of debts is not simply another way to speak of God's forgiveness of humankind. Rather, "forgiveness" or "release" in all arenas of human life is portrayed as one of the principal characteristics of humankind's encounter with God's reign. Building on the background of that term in the Jubilee traditions, one can see that it is in social, political, and economic arenas that the sovereignty of God finds its primary expression, breaking the stranglehold of the old order on those we have come to recognize as "the poor."

Four factors point to the importance of Jubilee traditions in establishing the meaning of forgiveness. First, the word *aphesis* referring to release from captivity does occur in Isa. 61:1, which is presented as the programmatic text for Jesus' ministry in Luke 4:18. Second, there is the influence on the Hebrew notion of forgiveness of the Greek meaning of *aphesis* as release from legal obligations. Third, these words are found in passages in the Gospels that refer literally to the forgiveness of debts, as well as in broader contexts. Finally, just as Jubilee traditions found in Second and Third Isaiah point to the release from bondage to the old order that will occur at the boundary of God's eschatological reign, so also in the Synoptic Gospels forgiveness is seen as an eschatological event. That event is linked to the proclamation and presence of Jesus in which the rule of all manner of evil is broken and the inauguration of God's reign becomes possible.

FORGIVENESS AND THE OUTCAST
(LUKE 7:36–50)

Each episode of Jesus' table community or other contact with outcasts and sinners can be seen as an enactment of "forgiveness." In these episodes, cultic and ethical barriers are overcome, and the person previously excluded finds herself or himself reincorporated into the community, and by extension reincorporated into the covenant relationship with God. Specific language about forgiveness, however, is rare in such episodes. One story in which both the language and the act of forgiveness play a role is the story of Jesus' anointing by a "woman of the city" at the home of a Pharisee (Luke 7:36–50).

The Pre-Gospel Development of the Story

Luke's version of the anointing story bears some resemblance to the story in Mark 14:3–9//Matt. 26:6–13 and John 12:1–8. They share such details as the setting at a meal, the host's name (Simon), the unusual anointing of Jesus by a woman, and the fact that the event led to controversy. Luke's version differs from the others in several details. First, Simon is identified as a Pharisee in Luke and as a leper in the Markan version. The woman is called "a sinner" by Luke, who portrays her as extremely agitated, whereas she neither receives that label nor exhibits that quality in the other Gospels. Matthew and Mark describe her as anointing Jesus' head, whereas Luke and John say she anoints his feet. Finally, the ensuing controversy in Luke turns on Jesus' word of forgiveness and his acceptance of the woman, whereas in the others she is upbraided for her wastefulness. These similarities and differences can be explained as reflecting two separate incidents in Jesus' life, or as two independent traditions concerning a single incident, or as the blending by Luke of details from the Markan anointing story with another story about an encounter between Jesus and a woman in which the theme was forgiveness. It is unlikely that Jesus would have been anointed by women twice during his ministry, and therefore the last two explanations seem more likely.

The two accounts may reflect separate traditions concerning a single event. In both accounts the incident itself is the context for a significant saying of Jesus. In the Markan account, both Jesus' praise of the woman's insight into the urgency of the moment and her response to Jesus in the context of the imminent passion are linked to the church's subsequent proclamation of the gospel. In Luke, the parable about forgiveness of debts (7:41–43), Jesus' declaration of the woman's forgiveness (7:47–48), and his statement about faith (7:50) provide an interpretation of the incident within the story itself. The two pronouncement stories with their different emphases may thus have emerged independently and been carried forward in Mark and the special Lukan material, respectively. Luke, then, may have chosen not to repeat the Markan story, having recognized its resemblance to the story that he had already presented in another form. It is possible to see how Luke, with his concern for the poor, might have been glad to omit Mark's account with what looks on the surface like Jesus' disregard for the disciples' advocacy for the poor. In presenting instead the other form of the anointing story, Luke would both have avoided Mark's ambiguous version and have presented another story of Jesus' intimate association with outcasts and his liberating intervention on their behalf.[3]

A more likely explanation of the Lukan anointing story, however, is that Luke himself, or the creator of the tradition on which he drew, has interwoven details from the Markan anointing story into a pronouncement story whose theme of forgiveness stems either from the parable in 7:41–43 or from the saying in 7:47. In fact, the anointing itself—which is the principal point of contact between the two accounts—is not central to Luke's story. The controversy in Luke's story turns not on the waste of the ointment or even on the specific act of anointing, but rather on the emotional extravagance of all of the woman's actions toward Jesus, his acceptance of them and of her, and the relationship between these actions and her being forgiven.[4]

The Nature of the Conflict

When the specific references to anointing (7:38 and 46) are removed, Luke's story is a conflict story set at a dinner in the home of a Pharisee. The conflict as Luke presents it has two points. The first and principal conflict is triggered by the arrival of the woman and Jesus' acceptance of her ministrations. Simon's implied hostility (7:39) is answered by Jesus' telling of the parable, the point of which the Pharisee recognizes (7:43). Jesus' point is then driven home by his application of the parable to what has occurred in Simon's house (7:44–45, 47), though the exact connection between the parable and the incident is difficult to discern.

The second point of conflict is introduced when Jesus turns to the woman herself with a declaration of forgiveness (Luke 7:48), which is followed by the questioning of the other guests (7:49) and Jesus' pronouncement of a blessing on the woman (7:50). These concluding verses of the story provide in an incident attributed to Jesus' lifetime a basis for the church's subsequent pronouncement of forgiveness in Jesus' name. Both in the declaration of forgiveness and in the people's response, this aspect of the conflict resembles the conflict occurring in the story of the healing of the person who was paralyzed (Matt. 9:2b–3//Mark 2:5–7//Luke 5:20–21). The words of blessing in Luke 7:50

echo the concluding words of healing stories such as Mark 10:52//Luke 18:42; Matt. 9:22//Mark 5:34//Luke 8:48; and Luke 17:19. These similarities to other passages suggest once again editorial work by which Luke or the formulators of his source gave a particular accent to the main pronouncement story.

The Woman's Story Unfolds

The setting in which the conflict takes place is tersely and vividly described. The meal in the home of a Pharisee is interrupted by the arrival of a woman identified as "a sinner" (7:37). Traditional interpretation of the story has assumed that because of that designation she must be a prostitute. Although she might have been called a sinner for many reasons, several details in the description of the woman and of her actions support that assumption. First, there is the disgrace of her unbound hair (7:38). Second, she appears to be on her own and not bound to her husband's household. Third, she not only has the expensive ointment with her, but apparently has the right to dispose of it.[5]

The woman's effusive behavior, compounded by the disgrace of her unbound hair, is presented by Luke without explanation. That lack of comment has prompted extensive debate about how Luke intended his readers to understand her motivation. The interpretation of her actions is linked, in turn, with the problem of understanding the relationship between love and forgiveness in the final form of the story. Ought one to conclude that her actions are motivated by contrition and thus are the basis on which her sins are declared forgiven? Or ought one to conclude that the incident and parable make the same point, namely, that her actions are the loving acts evoked and made possible by her knowledge of having already been forgiven?

The parable with which Jesus answers Simon's implied response to the woman and to Jesus' acceptance of her touch (7:41–42) is presented as a self-evident riddle. The very obviousness of the riddle traps Simon and evokes from him the response that will be his undoing (7:43). The parable refers to two debts of different amounts, both of which are forgiven *(charizomai)*. The question is which of the debtors will love the creditor more? Simon's response is the obvious one: the debtor whose canceled debt was larger. The point made in the parable is that one's expression of gratitude is related to a benefit

already received. The parable thus appears to support the interpretation of the woman's presence and actions as expressions of gratitude
rather than of penitence. The comparison of the woman's lavish
attention to Jesus with Simon's failure to have done more than the
absolute minimum required of him as a host (7:44–46) implies that
her actions grow out of her recognition of the gift of forgiveness that
she has received.

The summary statement in 7:47b also suggests that love or gratitude is a consequence of forgiveness. The present tense of the verbs in
that saying points to a general rule or proverbial truth, in contrast
with the perfect and aorist tenses of the preceding clause (7:47a).
There Jesus makes a specific declaration to the Pharisee about the
woman. The perfect tense of the reference to forgiveness would refer
to a condition in effect as a result of past action, and not to something
Jesus does at that moment. The aorist tense referring to the woman's
actions, on the other hand, does seem to refer to the specific deeds
that she has performed in the context of this story.

Both the parable and the saying in 7:47b help to clarify the problems of interpretation presented by 7:47a. Grammatically, v. 47a can
be understood to speak of love as either the cause or the evidence of
forgiveness. At issue is how one punctuates the sentence and how one
understands the introductory words *hou charin* ("therefore") and *hoti*
("for"). The sentence could mean "I tell you, therefore, that her
many sins are forgiven because she loved much." In that case, forgiveness would be the consequence of the love she has shown. It
could equally well mean, "For this reason I tell you that her sins are
forgiven, namely, that she loved much." Following that interpretation,
her loving actions would be evidence that she has already been
forgiven. The evidence of the parable in 7:41–43 and the saying in
7:47b, supported by the story context, suggests that Luke intended
the latter interpretation.

In this pericope, then, the woman who is called "a sinner" is
portrayed as having experienced forgiveness and as having recognized
that event to be linked to Jesus. In the pericope itself only the
pronouncement to the woman in 7:48 gives any suggestion that the
forgiveness was effected during the encounter. Even there the perfect
tense of the verb suggests that the forgiveness has already taken
place, though we are not told on what basis or when it happened. In

any case, there is no suggestion that it was necessarily preceded by any acts or declaration of penitence by the woman.

For the early church, however, her turning in gratitude to Jesus would indeed have been a sign of conversion or turning toward God. The events of repentance and forgiveness or of turning toward God and experiencing release from the bondage of sin are a summary of the woman's encounter with Jesus. The story itself, however, bears a different message by virtue of the social and political imagery in which it is cast.

In addition to describing a confrontation of Jesus with the self-righteousness of the host, this account also depicts Jesus' bridging of the gaps of social, religious, and ethical exclusivism by his association with outcasts and sinners. The story in Luke 7:36–50 makes explicit what is implicit elsewhere, namely, that in each case Jesus' relationship with the outcasts is to be understood as an enactment of the "forgiveness" or "release" in which those persons are restored to their place in the community. The bonds that are broken with Jesus' advent are the bonds that deprived people of a place in their society. Such pericopes echo the Jubilee images of "return" to God found in Leviticus 25 as well as those in Isaiah 61 that point to liberation from captivity and celebration of God's eschatological reign, now recognized as present in Jesus.

FORGIVENESS AND HEALING
(MARK 2:1–12//MATT. 9:1–8//LUKE 5:17–26)

All the healing stories recorded in the Gospels might be seen as manifestations of the liberation that is part of the Jubilee in that they portray release from powers inimical to the eschatological reign of God. They also take place primarily, thought not exclusively, among the "poor." In first-century Palestine, faith in miracles was widespread among people in lower economic classes who did not have the money to pay for medical treatment. Miracle workers were the court of last resort even for the well-to-do who had been rendered desperate and often destitute by the course of expensive and ineffective efforts at healing. Elisabeth Schüssler Fiorenza concludes "Miracle-faith in Jesus is best understood as protest against bodily and political suffering. It gives courage to resist the life-destroying powers of one's society."[6]

In the account of the healing of the person who was paralyzed, however, physical healing or "release" from disease is explicitly linked to "release" or "forgiveness" of sins. Matthew and Luke appear to have followed Mark's version of this pericope with only minor editorial revisions.[7] Luke has also retained the Markan context of the pericope as the first in a collection of five conflict stories (Mark 2:1—3:6//Luke 5:17—6:11), and Matthew has kept the first three of these together (Matt. 9:1–17) before varying from Mark's order.

The introductory verses in Mark and Luke set the story in the context of a preaching or teaching event in which Jesus was surrounded by crowds, a detail corroborated within the story itself (Mark 2:4). The story is a complex account, including both a healing narrative and a conflict story centering on Jesus' sayings about forgiveness. The healing story by itself (Mark 2:3–5, 11–12) resembles many others in the Synoptic Gospels. It could stand on its own as a complete story. It includes the identification of the man's illness and the process by which he was brought to Jesus (2:3–4), Jesus' words declaring the fact of healing (2:11 and perhaps 2:5), evidence of the healing (2:12a), and the response of the crowd (2:12b).

It is not clear whether Mark 2:5b, referring to God's forgiveness of the man, should be seen as part of the healing story. That verse differs from 2:6–10, where the issue is Jesus' authority to forgive, perhaps reflecting a debate between the early church and the synagogue about the church's authority to declare forgiveness through Jesus. From a literary point of view, the suggestion that 2:5b be considered part of the original healing story makes sense, since it accounts for the means by which the conflict and healing stories were joined, namely, the motif of forgiveness. Furthermore, if the healing story including all of 2:5 does indeed reflect a reminiscence about a specific or typical event from Jesus' life, it suggests the uncomfortable possibility that Jesus accepted and acted within the contemporary belief structure that saw disease as a punishment for sin. While it would seem logical that Jesus as a person of his day would hold such views, it hardly seems like a picture of Jesus that the early church would want to invent. If the link of forgiveness and healing does go back to Jesus, such a link reinforces the connection between Jesus' *declaration* of forgiveness or release, and his *action* in which the release from bondage is effected.

The conflict portion of the story (Mark 2:6–10) could not have circulated independently in its present form, since it lacks a setting, a triggering event, and a conclusion. It is clear, therefore, that Mark or his source did not simply join two otherwise separate accounts. Three possibilities exist. First, the pericope may always have existed in a compound form, perhaps reflecting an actual or typical incident in Jesus' life in which words of forgiveness were pronounced in the context of a healing, and in which such words in turn provoked objections from the religious authorities. An argument against that possibility is the fact that the response of "all" the onlookers (2:12) does not seem a likely reaction of those who earlier had charged Jesus with blasphemy (2:7). A stronger argument against the original unity of this pericope is the fact that, whereas "faith" appears in 2:5 as the factor that enabled the healing, in the conflict portion healing is not associated with faith but with forgiveness. The two portions of the story thus appear to develop different theological principles and issues.

A second possibility by which to account for the present form of the pericope is that the conflict story existed in the oral tradition in complete form, as a story built on the *huios tou anthrōpou* saying in 2:10. When that story was combined with the healing story, its own beginning and ending would have been omitted, and details would have been added to link it more specifically to the healing story. If the healing story included the statement on forgiveness in 2:5b, it is easy to see how another story whose focus was forgiveness might have been joined to it, emphasizing that theme over the more traditional connection between healing and faith. In the pericope in its final form, however, details from the healing story (such as the reference to the paralyzed person and to the pallet on which he was brought) are interwoven with the conflict story (2:9–10). That fact would presuppose thorough editorial work within the supposedly separate conflict story, and not simply its insertion into the middle of the healing story as might be expected if the two accounts were originally independent of each other.

A third possibility, which might be seen as a variant of the second, is that Mark or the formulator of his source composed the conflict portion, perhaps building it around the saying in 2:10, in order to address the issue of the church's authority to forgive sins in Jesus' name. The conflict then would justify ecclesiastical practice, apparently by means of an argument from a major to a minor event (if the authority for the ostensibly more difficult healing is present, so must be the authority to forgive), but actually by appealing to the actions and authority of Jesus.

The third hypothesis is the most persuasive in that it leaves the fewest questions unanswered and requires the fewest assumptions about prior traditions or authors' motivations. Both the second and the third hypotheses account for the fact that not all of the major themes of the healing story are reflected in the conflict portion, as might be expected if the pericope were a unit or a reflection of a single incident. Unlike the second hypothesis, the third accounts for the interweaving of details from the healing story with the conflict story in 2:9-10, and provides a context within which the *huios tou anthrōpou* saying can be understood, namely, in the defense of the church's authority to forgive sins by appeal to Jesus' example and authority, without resorting to further assumptions about the authenticity or historicity of various types of such sayings.

If it is the case, then, that the healing story in 2:3-5, 11-12 is the core around which Mark or his source has built the pericope, that core provides evidence of traditions concerning Jesus' healing ministry and also evidence linking that aspect of Jesus' ministry with the motif of forgiveness. That connection appears to have been so significant that Mark could develop a defense of the church's ministry to mediate God's forgiveness on the basis of an argument that Jesus' power over physical paralysis was linked to his authority over sin.

FORGIVENESS OF DEBTS

A further clue to the meaning of forgiveness in Jesus' message can be found in the image of cancellation of debts. The issue of forgiveness is expressed in terms of that image in two contexts: the parable of the Unforgiving Servant (Matt. 18:21-35) and the petition concerning forgiveness in the Lord's Prayer and related sayings (Matt. 6:12//Luke 11:4; Matt. 6:14-15//Mark 11:25-26).

The Parable of the Unforgiving Servant
(Matt. 18:21-35)

The parable of the Unforgiving Servant is found only in Matthew and is marked by Matthean vocabulary and style. It is likely that the parable came from Matthew's special source (M), or else that it was subsequently reworked by Matthew.[8] It is found at the end of a collection of teachings introduced by a discussion among the disciples about who is the greatest in God's realm (Matt. 18:1). Matthew follows Mark for much of that discussion (Matt. 18:1–9//Mark 9:33–50), then incorporates additional material (Matt. 18:10–35).

In the course of the dispute about greatness, Mark and Matthew both present a catechetical primer of sayings linked by catchwords and by the theme of advice about conduct in the community of Jesus' followers. Matthew speaks in 18:2–4 of "a child" *(paidion)* as one on whom the disciples are to model themselves in their relationship to God's reign, and as one to be received in Jesus' name. In 18:6, *ta paidia* becomes "the little ones" *(hoi mikroi)* who are not to be "caused to stumble" *(skandalizō)*. In 18:7–9, the dangers of being "led to stumble" by one's hand, foot, or eye are described, but instead of embroidering further the theme of "fire" as does Mark (Mark 9:49–50), Matthew returns to the theme of the "little ones" and their importance, as the introduction and conclusion to the parable of the Lost Sheep (Matt. 18:10, 14). Matthew 18:15 changes the theme only slightly from the "little ones" to one's "brother" (which here appears to refer to a member of the community and not to a sibling), and from the subject of "causing a little one to perish" to that of "sinning." The issue of the means of intrachurch discipline of the one who sins (Matt. 18:15–20) merges into the theme of forgiveness of the other (18:21–22). Forgiveness is then further interpreted, not in sayings about human behavior, but in the imagery of a parable of God's reign (18:23–35).

The saying about forgiveness in Matt. 18:21–22 is different from its parallel in Luke 17:4. In Luke, the counsel that one must forgive whenever the offender repents is extremely demanding on human relationships, but nevertheless it is a realistic guide for daily behavior. Matthew presents the saying not as a teaching initiated by Jesus, but as Jesus' response to Peter's question about the limits of one's obligation to forgive another. Jesus' response suggests a total number of occasions of forgiveness that is so large[9] that keeping a tally would obviously be absurd. What Matthew suggests by this hyperbole and by the parable that follows is that forgiveness is not simply a function of ethical obligation, but is an expression of God's reign in the very fabric of human community and social relationships.

The parable bears evidence of the storyteller's art and imagination in the elevated position of the characters—a king and his satrap—and in the contrast between the huge debt owed by the satrap and the paltry sum owed to him.[10] Although the king is the first character mentioned, the satrap is the principal character, whom the story follows from despair, to promise, to being even worse off than at first.[11] At the beginning of the story his debt is larger than he could ever hope to repay, and therefore his request for additional time must be seen as an act of desperation. The king's response is the only one that could have helped the servant, namely, the cancellation of the entire debt.

Coming on the heels of the king's action, the servant's response to his colleague is even more offensive. His petitioner's words are an exact echo of his own plea to the king, and the satrap's response is to deny even what may be a reasonable request for additional time to repay the small debt.[12] Learning of the satrap's action, the king responds in a way that makes the point of the parable clear: because the servant has not shown mercy, his own debt is reinstated, and he is imprisoned without hope of release. The new freedom inaugurated by the king's initial canceling of his debt is now denied to the satrap, who wants only its benefits and not the task of continuing that pattern in his relationships with others in an economy characterized by mercy and forgiveness.

The argument of the king is not an argument from the greater to the lesser, emphasizing the respective sizes of the two debts. Instead, the two opportunities for mercy are equated. The point of the story is not that people should always be forgiving of one another because of the infinite scope of God's forgiveness of humankind, compared with which any human "debts" would be insignificant. Similarly, the point is not the meting out of reward and punishment by an external authority. The point is rather to portray the choices now possible concerning the rules by which one's life is to be governed, and the consequences of choosing the old order over the new. Being willing to receive forgiveness for one's own debts, but not to forgive others in turn, is in effect to deny the new economy of mercy in favor of the old one in which the bonds and obligations leading to indebtedness still hold sway.

Matthew introduces this parable as if it were the consequence of (*dia touto*) the preceding saying about forgiveness (18:22). Thus the saying itself envisions a new reign or order in which receiving the message of "release" or "forgiveness" as both a gift and an obligation is a condition of one's participation. If the parable simply *illustrated* that saying, it would follow that the satrap ought to be forgiven even for his failure to forgive the other servant. Instead, the parable interprets the saying by placing it in the context of God's reign, the onset of which is marked by forgiveness and release from the patterns of debt and obligation by which the old order is maintained. Human resistance to living with the consequences of that cancellation of old patterns is not an unforgivable sin. Rather it constitutes a self-exclusion from God's reign and from the life characterized by mercy and liberation that is its hallmark.

Sayings About Forgiveness of Debts
(Matt. 6:12//Luke 11:4; Matt. 6:14–15//Mark 11:25–26)

The motif of forgiveness of debts is found also in the second "we" petition of the Lord's Prayer (Matt. 6:12//Luke 11:4) and in similar sayings found elsewhere in Matthew and Mark. These sayings establish a connection between God's forgiveness of humankind and people's forgiveness of each other. Understanding the nature of that connection requires that one look at the relationship between the words "sins" and "debts," and at the expressions by which Matthew and Luke link the two halves of the petition of the Lord's Prayer. Matthew's version of the petition presents the related words "debts" *(ta opheilēmata)* and "debtors" *(tois opheiletais)* in the two halves of the petition. Luke has similar language in the participial form of the verb *opheilō* in the apodosis, but breaks the parallelism by referring to "sins" *(tas hamartias)* in the protasis.

The verb *opheilō* and nouns related to it do not occur often in the Synoptic Gospels, and when they do they usually refer to an economic or other legal obligation (Matt. 18:24–34; 23:16, 18; Luke 7:41; 13:4; 16:5, 7; 17:10). The problem of accounting for the introduction of "sins" in Luke, or in the version of the Lord's Prayer on which he drew, begins to be resolved in the face of proposed reconstructions of a possible Hebrew or Aramaic version of the petition. The two pairs of terms usually proposed in such reconstructions, *ḥôb/ ḥōba* and *nešî/maššâ'âh*, have both a financial and a more general ethical meaning: they refer to "debts" and to "sins."[13] Whether or not Matthew and Luke were aware of those two levels of meaning, both are represented in each of their versions of the prayer. Luke represents both within the petition of the prayer. Matthew introduces the

word "trespasses" *(paraptōmata)*, which is another possible translation of the Semitic words, in the expansion of the petition in 6:14–15
after having referred to "debts" and "debtors" in the prayer.

With respect to the wording of the prayer itself, it is reasonable to
assume that both Matthew and Luke drew on the liturgical traditions
of their communities. The fact that Matt. 6:14–15//Mark 11:25–26
represents the only occurrence of the word "trespasses" in the Synoptic Gospels suggests that Matthew may have drawn those verses from
the saying in Mark. Matthew appears to have expanded that saying
into two parallel statements, one positive and one negative, about the
interrelationship of divine and human forgiveness.[14] For Matthew,
then, the Markan saying interprets the ethical implications of the
petition of the preceding prayer. That meaning was already present in
Luke's version of the prayer, and that fact may account for his omission of the Markan saying.

The tradition of focusing on the parallel between "debts" and "sins"
or "trespasses" in the petition of the Lord's Prayer has led to the
suggestion that the petition rests on an argument from the greater to
the lesser. According to that interpretation, we are required to pardon the lesser offenses committed against us by other people because
God's forgiveness of us is so much greater. Related to this interpretation have been various theories of atonement that point to the Christ
as the one in whom the "debt" of human sin was either canceled or
paid in full. Then, because that ultimate debt against us has been
satisfied, we are obliged to pardon others.

The grammar of both versions of the petition, however, suggests a
problem with that interpretation. The problem centers on the con-
junctions by which the writers introduce the second half of the
petition. Matthew's "as also" *(hōs kai)*, followed by a verb in the
aorist tense, suggests either a resemblance in manner or a propor-
tional relationship between the forgiveness being asked of God and
what the person praying either has done or is doing. Luke's "for also"
(kai gar), followed by a verb in the present tense, sounds as though
the pattern of human behavior is to be either the model, the rationale, or even the cause of God's forgiving response. Neither version of the petition supports the traditional argument from the
greater act of God to the lesser obligation for humankind, and the
meaning of each version by itself is puzzling. On grammatical

grounds, therefore, the petition leaves the problem of the relationship between divine and human forgiveness unresolved.

The way out of the dilemma posed by this petition is to restore it to the context of the whole prayer. Since the Lord's Prayer is a prayer for God's reign to be established, the petition concerning forgiveness needs to be seen in relationship to that reign. The issue is similar to that posed by the parable in Matt. 18:23–35 where God's reign is associated with patterns or rhythms of forgiveness as both gift and mandate. In the Lord's Prayer also, therefore, one's prayer for God's reign includes a petition for an "economy" characterized by forgiveness, and a statement of one's determination to participate in that economy as one who is both forgiver and forgiven.

Those persons who would hear such a word as "good news" are clearly those for whom "debts," whether before God or to other persons, result in a captivity that denies the fullness of life. Among them would surely be the people considered outcasts by their neighbors, with whom Jesus so often enjoyed table community. Among them too would be those ensnared in the vicious cycle of literal indebtedness in the struggle to make of less-than-subsistence wages an adequate livelihood. The image of God's reign as beginning precisely in the breaking of that dehumanizing pattern supports the theological affirmation that God is in fact claiming sovereignty over all of life, and that the advent of God's reign is indeed an event of liberation at the most basic level of human life.[15]

Those for whom such a word would be bad news are equally easy to recognize. In religious terms, they would be those committed to a life of righteousness and obedience to religious requirements codified in Torah or in Christian tradition. In social and political terms, they would be those who profit from the patterns of indebtedness that characterize business as usual. Those "debts" are both the literal economic ones and also the dehumanizing patterns of obligation inherent in social roles and in categories defining one's participation in social and political institutions. In other words, the privileged people would have their pretense to status confronted and their self-made security threatened.

For those people, the Lord's Prayer would be a difficult one, because as a prayer for God's reign to be established, it affirms the fact that between the human present and God's future comes a proclamation of "release." The petition concerning the "forgiveness of debts" portrays in a condensed and economical way the radical change in relationships and behavior that is both required and made possible in the reign of God proclaimed by Jesus the Christ.

CHAPTER 6

Jubilee Images
Interwoven

The Lord's Prayer and
Summary Statements About Jesus

The images of "release" or "forgiveness," of "good news to the poor," and of Jesus as herald of God's reign are interwoven in the many summary statements defining Jesus' significance and providing transitional passages in the gospel story. Those same images come together also in the Lord's Prayer. This collection of texts completes the picture that has been evolving of the role of Jubilee images in ethics and Christology in the Synoptic Gospels. It is also the final piece of data underlying the critical and historical-theological conclusions on which a contemporary response can be based.

THE LORD'S PRAYER AS
A JUBILEE PRAYER

Matthew and Luke present slightly different versions of the prayer taught by Jesus. The two versions may reflect different occasions when Jesus taught a similar prayer to the disciples and other hearers, or separate traditions recalling a single occasion and prayer. The differences may also stem from adaptations of a common tradition of that prayer by one or both of the Gospel writers for stylistic or theological reasons, or to reflect the liturgical practice of a particular community. The last possibility seems the most likely. Such aesthetic considerations as the cadence and parallelism of the petitions of Matthew's prayer point more clearly to a liturgical context than does Luke's simpler form. On the other hand, Luke's use of present instead of aorist imperatives in the first two petitions that occur in the first person plural ("give us each day our daily bread," and "forgive us our sins") seem to relate the prayer to the ongoing life of a community such as that to which Luke wrote, and to deemphasize the eschatological tone that it has in Matthew. Luke's version of the prayer manifests further redaction in the petition for forgiveness, where both "sins" and "debts" are joined in the petition of the prayer itself.[1]

The prayer divides naturally into two parts. In the first part, the petitions are directed toward God's activity in general (the so-called thou petitions), and in the second part the petitions have in view specific human concerns (the "we" petitions). The first group of petitions represents the prayer that God's eschatological reign be established, and the second group addresses human concerns and experiences anticipated in connection with that reign.

Luke presents two "thou" petitions: "may thy name be hallowed" and "may thy reign come." Matthew has a third: "may thy will be done."[2] All three of these petitions are related to the motif of divine sovereignty. For God's name to be hallowed would mean that the glory of the name itself, and hence the glory of its bearer, would be revealed. That glory is often identified with God's power that works liberation and redemption for God's people, and in that sense it is also related to the establishment of God's reign.[3] The second of the common petitions is specifically a prayer for the advent of God's reign. Matthew's parallel petition referring to God's will reinforces the image of God as active sovereign, with heaven and earth together as the sphere of God's authority. Matthew's petition expresses not merely submission to God's greater power but also consent to a comprehensive fulfillment of God's will, in keeping with the hallowing of the name and the establishment of God's reign. It expresses not a feeling of resignation, but a turning toward God with hope and longing.[4]

The petition for bread is the first of the "we" petitions. It is puzzling both because of the word *epiousios*, of which the meaning is unclear, and because of the differences in verb tense and wording between the two versions. Whatever the exact meaning of the adjective *epiousios*,[5] the "bread" appears to refer to that which sustains or redeems life, and for which humankind must count on God's providence. It thus has echoes of both the bread of the messianic banquet and the manna by which the Israelites were sustained in their journey through the wilderness (Exod. 16:4; Ps. 78:24). The bread calls to mind both God's gift of eschatological fullness and God's constant daily presence and care for the people.[6]

The final common petition of the prayer (along with Matthew's additional one) must also be understood in the context of the focus of the prayer on the moment of anticipation and of transition, when God's eschatological reign is still prayed for, but when the events marking its impact on human experience are already proclaimed. The "temptation," or more accurately "testing" *(ho peirasmos)*, would then refer to the time of trial traditionally associated with the onset of the end time, and the "Evil One" (or "Evil" in the sense of a virtually personified power) would refer to the one with whom the ultimate battle for sovereignty is waged.[7]

Although it is clear that the Lord's Prayer is thoroughly eschatological in emphasis, the specific question that remains is the extent to which this prayer can legitimately be called a Jubilee prayer. The language and imagery of the petition for forgiveness of debts are clearly associated with Jubilee traditions. That petition alone, however, does not warrant interpreting the whole prayer in light of those traditions. Rather, the remaining petitions must be examined for evidence of Jubilee images as well. The first three petitions, addressing the establishment of God's reign and will, are not expressed in language exclusively related to Jubilee traditions. On the other hand, their focus on the advent of God's reign is appropriate to Jubilee traditions, among others, insofar as Jubilee images elsewhere in the Synoptic Gospels are part of the inaugural proclamation associated with God's reign.

The "we" petitions might be expected to conform more closely to Jubilee categories, in that these petitions focus on the human side of the advent of God's reign, even as elsewhere in the Gospels Jubilee images address the human experience of an encounter with the proclamation of that reign. The petition for bread does not have direct parallels in any of the phrases of Isa. 61:1-2, and therefore cannot be considered to be direct evidence of the influence of Jubilee traditions as found in Hebrew Scriptures. The question, however, cannot be dismissed that quickly, for the messianic banquet as a metaphor for the reign of God has already been encountered in passages elaborating on "good news to the poor," particularly in Luke 14. Furthermore, this petition of the prayer echoes other passages related to Isa. 61:1-2, such as the Beatitudes which include the blessing of food for the hungry as one of the manifestations of God's reign. Thus, even though the petition for bread does not reflect primarily the Jubilee traditions, it is nevertheless consistent with them, and especially with the announcement of "good news to the poor."

The final petition of Luke's version of the prayer and the last two of Matthew's reflect other traditions associated with God's eschatological victory. Only by tenuous connections might these be linked to the notion of God's reign. These petitions cannot, therefore, be enlisted as evidence for the Jubilee character of the prayer, but they can be noted as being consistent with the general eschatological thrust of the prayer.

In summary, the Lord's Prayer is an eschatological prayer that resembles other places in the Synoptic Gospels where the advent of God's reign is portrayed in images reminiscent of the Jubilee traditions in Hebrew Scriptures. In the prayer, petitions for God's reign to be established are followed by others addressed to people's anticipation of the implications of that reign, just as in the Jubilee traditions of Hebrew Scriptures affirmations of God's activity and sovereignty are followed by statements about human responsibility. The focus of the prayer is thus on the boundary moment, the point of change from the old order to the new. While the reign prayed for is clearly God's reign, and not something evolving from human actions, its advent implies consequences for human beings and for human society. Those consequences include the need to participate in the rhythms of "forgiveness," and response to the "good news to the poor" symbolized in the petition for bread. While it is therefore not appropriate to call the Lord's Prayer a Jubilee prayer in the strict sense of being able to trace each of its petitions to specific Jubilee texts, it is a Jubilee prayer in that it expresses, in a highly condensed and symbolic liturgical form, images in common with the Jubilee traditions of Hebrew Scriptures as elaborated elsewhere in the Synoptic Gospels.

SUMMARY STATEMENTS ABOUT JESUS

All three Synoptic Gospels contain summary statements in which Jubilee themes and images are interwoven. These statements, probably provided by the Gospel writers themselves, form literary bridges between individual pericopes and larger units drawn from various sources. Despite considerable variety of detail, these transitional, introductory, and concluding statements give evidence of the customary combination of certain terms and types of activity to summarize Jesus' message and ministry. The summary statements usually include a reference to the reign of God, either as the direct object of verbs of proclamation or as part of what is labeled as Jesus' "proclamation" or "good news." Healings or the casting out of demons are also often mentioned as evidence of the transformative power of that reign. In all but one of the statements where there is no reference to healing or exorcism, the themes of "repentance" or "forgiveness" occur. By joining references to the proclamation of the reign of God with references to Jesus' actions and words of "release" from various forms of bondage or indebtedness, these summary statements echo the Jubilee themes found in Isa. 61:1–2, especially as these are represented in other pericopes of the Synoptic Gospels.

Whether any of the Gospel writers was aware of perpetuating Jubilee traditions in such summary statements is highly doubtful, particularly as their work became more widely removed from the thought-world of ancient Palestine and from the traditions found in Hebrew Scriptures. These statements appear instead to have served the purpose of encapsulating what the Gospel writers and the compilers of their sources understood to have been Jesus' message and significance for his own day and for the early church. These statements may also reflect ways in which Jesus himself summarized his work, namely, as herald of God's eschatological reign. Of course neither that possibility nor any conclusion about the awareness by the Gospel writers of the Jubilee roots of these images can be established with certainty.

The frequency and location of the summary statements containing Jubilee images, and the specific images that each statement contains, are indicated in table 1. In Matthew and Mark, all of these statements occur prior to the account of Peter's confession at Caesarea Philippi (Matt. 16:23//Mark 8:27–33//Luke 9:18–22). In Luke, three occur after that pericope. This may indicate that such summary statements were understood by Mark and Matthew to be suitable representations of the earlier part of Jesus' ministry, until his christological identity came to be more fully defined. Luke, on the other hand, seems to find it appropriate to carry such summaries throughout the Gospel.

All three Synoptic Gospels link such summary statements not only to Jesus, but also to the work of John the Baptist and of the disciples. The association of such statements with the work of the disciples is

TABLE 1

Summary Statements with Jubilee Images

Key: Jubilee Images

a. "the reign of God"
b. "to proclaim good news" *(euaggelizomai)*
c. "the proclamation of good news" *(euaggelion)*
d. "to proclaim" *(kēryssō)*

e. healing
f. exorcism
g. "release" or "forgiveness"
h. "to repent"
i. "repentance"

Passages	Images
Matt. 3:2[1,5]	a, h
4:17	a, d, h
4:23	a, c, d, e
9:35	a, c, d, e
10:7[2]	a, d, e
12:28[5]	a, f
Mark 1:14–15	a, c, d, h
1:39	d, f
3:14–15[2]	d, f
6:12–13[3]	d, e, f
Luke 4:43	a, b, d
8:1	a, b, d, e, f
9:1–2[2]	a, d, e, f
9:6[3]	b, e
9:11	a, d ("to speak"), e
10:9[4,5]	a, e
11:20[5]	a, f
24:47	d, g, i

[1]Refers to the ministry of John the Baptist.
[2]Refers to the commission given to the Twelve.
[3]Summarizes the missionary work of the Twelve.
[4]Refers to the commission given to the Seventy.
[5]Places where there are no words of proclamation associated with the "reign of God," but where the saying itself is an announcement or proclamation.

particularly significant in Luke, where they occur three times in conjunction with the activity of the disciples during Jesus' lifetime and are part of the instructions (Luke 24:47) of the risen Christ to the "eleven . . . and those with them" (Luke 24:33). Luke links such themes more explicitly to the mission of the early church, both in summary statements of the church's kerygma and in particular sermons attributed to the apostles in the Book of Acts (1:3; 2:38; 3:19; 5:30–31, 42; 8:12; 10:34–43; 13:32, 38–39; 14:7; 26:16–18). The themes of "repentance" and "forgiveness" that are found in Luke 24:47 also occur frequently in Acts, where "forgiveness" is associated with the person or name of Jesus.[8]

The reign of God is mentioned in only one of the summary statements in Mark, but it is often found in the parallel verses in Matthew and Luke. Why Mark would not have included it is difficult to say, since he was clearly well acquainted with its prominence in Jesus' preaching. Its occurrence in the parallel verses seems to reflect Matthew and Luke's awareness that the reign of God was indeed the focus of Jesus' attention and therefore belonged in a summary of his activity and importance. Perhaps they inserted references to God's reign in order to make that focus clear, and at the same time to bring the Markan statements into harmony with their own summaries found elsewhere.

In none of the summary statements is any content given to the phrase "the reign of God." It is simply "preached" *(kēryssō)* or "proclaimed as good news" *(euaggelizomai)*. Just as in the parables that point to God's reign with imaginative or symbolic language, or capture the drama of God's reign in collision with the predictability of the old order, so also in these summary statements it is the fact of God's sovereignty, rather than any limiting description of its nature, that is important. The newness and freedom of God's activity remains uncircumscribed. By focusing in the summary statements on the proclamation or imminence of God's reign, the evangelists keep their readers' attention on people's experience when they encounter God's reign. In that way they emphasize the events that mark the end of the old order in the deeds and proclamation of the herald who declares the inauguration of God's reign in which all things are made new.

CONCLUSION

The evidence assembled in this and the preceding three chapters has shown that passages containing Jubilee images are found in all four of the generally recognized sources of the Synoptic Gospels (Mark, Q, M, and L), and in summary statements that are probably the contributions of the Gospel writers themselves.[9] Of these sources, Q contains the largest number of passages with Jubilee images. Luke not only contains a larger number of such passages than either Mark or Matthew, but those passages are given further prominence by their place in the Gospel, such as in the inaugural portrait of Jesus (Luke 4:16–30) and in the commission from the risen Christ (Luke 24:47). In addition to occurring in all of the sources and in the contributions of the evangelists, Jubilee images have been shown to occur in a variety of forms within the larger sources. These images form the core sayings in several pronouncement stories and are found in parables, in the Lord's Prayer, and in several teaching passages. They also figure in accounts of Jesus' table community with outcasts and sinners.

This evidence supports the conclusion that it appears quite likely that Jubilee images figured in the teachings and ministry of Jesus himself. Despite the breadth of attestation of such images, however, what can be known about *how* Jubilee images figured in Jesus' ministry is severely limited. The Gospels do not provide evidence of any particular event in which one can be certain that Jesus actually presented a Jubilee program as part of his agenda. There is no evidence that Jesus identified a particular calendar year as a Jubilee year according to the pattern of Leviticus 25.

All of Jesus' message and activity can, of course, not be forced into a Jubilee mold, as though that were the only set of guiding images of his ministry. One would also not be warranted in assuming that Jesus deliberately used Jubilee images to interpret for the disciples, for his opponents, or for onlookers the events in which he participated. In fact, one cannot be certain that Jesus was aware that the images of "good news to the poor" and of "release" or "forgiveness" were associated with Jubilee traditions. He may rather have included these simply on the basis of their role in Isa. 61:1–2 and related passages pointing to the transformation associated with God's reign.

It is precisely in the context of his announcement of the reign of God that Jesus' message of "good news to the poor" and of "release" from enslavement to old authorities—in other words, his proclamation of a Jubilee—should be understood. Insofar as Jesus recognized that God's eschatological reign was at hand, he apparently summoned people to affirm God's authority and sovereign will. To do so meant to respond first of all to the edict that spelled good news and blessing to various groups related to "the poor," and release from the various forms of enslavement to rules, powers, and authorities belonging in the old age. The message brought by Jesus to mark the experience of humankind at the near boundary of God's reign was in *fact,* if not necessarily in conscious *intent,* a Jubilee message. As such, it had the effect of pronouncing sentence on the powers preventing the exercise of God's new reign, which would touch, transform, and redeem the whole created order.

As difficult as it is to know how and to what extent the Jubilee proclamation was deliberately chosen and recognized as such by Jesus, it is equally difficult to know whether the Gospel writers or their sources were aware of incorporating images rooted in the Jubilee traditions, or whether they simply reproduced such images without being aware of their roots. It is clear, however, that the presence of those images was persuasive or pervasive enough that they were preserved in all the Synoptic Gospels, and that they figured prominently in the identification and definition of Jesus as the Christ, especially though not exclusively in the Gospel of Luke.

Nevertheless, the christological designation of "herald" of God's reign, which would be appropriate to such images, was apparently not considered by the early church to be an adequate designation of Jesus. Although the role of herald emphasizes the identity and authority as well as the task of the messenger, for the community formed and empowered in the event of the resurrection, Jesus' own story came to be proclaimed as the content of the gospel. Even in that process by which the proclaimer became more explicitly the one proclaimed, however, Jubilee themes were not lost, and the message of liberation became part of the proclamation of Jesus as the Christ.

What appears to have occurred is a three-step process. First, Jubilee images and traditions appear to have played a major role in Jesus' own activity and message. In the second step of the process, the early church, prompted and focused by the Easter experience that gave it birth, drew on a variety of images associated with Jesus' own message in order to proclaim Jesus' identity as the Christ and his saving significance for all believers. Later on, as the early church built the traditions concerning Jesus' life and ministry into the Gospel accounts, Jubilee references again appeared more explicitly. By then those images carried a double significance, including both their original connection to Jesus' proclamation of God's reign and their subsequent role in the christological confession of the early church.

In conclusion, then, whatever specific form the gospel takes, it encounters humankind as the proclamation of "good news" and "release" heralding God's eschatological reign. That proclamation entails the demand that one face God's reign without the limitations, securities, and self-definitions that make the old order at once oppressive and familiar. The Jubilee message is thus good news to those who know themselves to be dependent on God's grace and not on their own powers, and a word of judgment to those unable or unwilling to share in its rhythms of release and liberation. The particular message of that gospel to us requires a careful hearing, with courage where it frightens us, and gentleness where it sets us free, in the name of the Christ and for the sake of the sovereign God.

CHAPTER 7

In Christ
We Are Set Free

Jubilee Images Re-encountered

The task of moving from the biblical Jubilee images to their implications for contemporary theological reflection and response requires a delicate probing of the images in their own settings in the early church, and perhaps in Jesus' own ministry, and then careful listening for their contemporary echoes. That task is complex. To attempt to draw simple, direct, or literal connections between the Jubilee traditions of the Bible and contemporary situations of pain or of human need is not a legitimate approach for several reasons. First, to do so would be a violation of the historical particularity of those texts. Second, it would represent a distortion of the way in which these traditions meet us as images, and thus evoke responses and reorient our perspective rather than prescribing solutions. Finally, it would deny the focus of Jubilee imagery on the boundary moments when life of human design encounters the reality of God's sovereign will for humankind. All three of these words of hermeneutical caution in our approach to Jubilee traditions have as a consequence the fact that the task of interpretation is ongoing. It is never completed once for all times, nor is it done in one place for people in all social locations.

However, while it would be illegitimate and even impossible for us to attempt to say once and for all what the Jubilee images found in the Bible mean for contemporary theological discussion, or where they call people to invest their energy in today's world, we are nevertheless not rendered mute on these issues. Rather, many responses to Jubilee images, coming from persons in various cultural and social contexts, are needed to open up both the ancient texts and their contemporary meanings. The previous chapters of this study which probe the biblical Jubilee traditions with the help of the disciplines of critical scholarship, as well as the following attempt to discern the contemporary implications of these traditions, must be understood as but a single voice in the conversation. Other persons in different contexts will encounter and respond to the Jubilee images in quite different ways.

As a provisional conclusion to the study, however, I would like to offer some reflections on five issues related to the Jubilee images of the Synoptic Gospels that seem to me either problematic or potentially helpful for contemporary ethical or christological reflection. These five issues are christological language and imagery, the agenda of "justice," forgiveness and liberation, the affirmation of divine sovereignty, and the relationship between the eschatology of the Jubilee and ethical responsibility.

THE CHRIST AS HERALD OF THE JUBILEE

("The Spirit of God is upon me, for God has anointed me")

The image of the Christ as herald of the Jubilee suggests several implications for christological reflection. First of all, the Christology underlying the Jubilee images is at its heart theocentric. The royal herald calls attention to the sovereign who follows in the procession. The herald's authority derives from the commission to represent and speak for the sovereign, not from any quality belonging to the messenger alone. Thus, the relationship between Christ and God is portrayed as a very intimate one, and at the same time one in which the accent is not on the particular human characteristics of the Christ—gender, ethnic identity, or historical situation. Barriers of exclusivism are thus minimized, and the function or activity in which Jesus is recognized as the Christ comes into focus.

Second, in that focus the images of the Jubilee traditions highlight the fact that in Christ people are met by the healing, freeing, redeeming presence of God at their points of greatest pain. The redemptive work of Christ is depicted as touching all of human life. The Jubilee images point toward God's liberating and healing intent wherever institutions, customs, or physical conditions are seen to limit human life. Divisions between sacred and secular are removed. The political, economic, and social realities of life do not provide mere illustrations of the way in which God's reign is experienced. Rather they are identified as the precise arenas where the impact of God's reign is felt.

As noted above, the theocentric focus of the Jubilee traditions diminishes the role of the human attributes of Jesus as barriers separating the Christ from human beings of other places, times, or gender. On the other hand, however, the historical and cultural particularity of Jesus and of the Gospel writers are important precisely because the Jubilee traditions are developed by concrete images. A third point to note, then, as one looks to the Jubilee traditions in one's christological reflection, is that this historical and cultural relativity functions not to limit the applicability of the gospel message or the importance of the Christ, but rather to ground them in actual historical circumstances. We can, of course, not be certain of particular events or words in which Jesus of Nazareth carried forward the Jubilee message. It is nevertheless significant that an actual human being was the bearer of this Jubilee message, and embodied its revolutionary openness to God's intent in a fully human life and context. The one who meets us as herald of the Jubilee of God's reign does so in the particular historical, social, and economic circumstances of his time, just as we are responsible for recognizing and responding to the same message in the midst of our own historical and cultural particularity. The message is no safe one, confined to an otherworldly or religious sphere of life, but rather strikes us now, as it did those who first heard it, in the midst of the institutions and assumptions by which our lives are organized.

THE AGENDA OF JUSTICE

("To proclaim good news to the poor")

In the Jubilee traditions, God's reign is heralded by "good news to the poor." "The poor" are linked to such other persons as those who are blind, maimed, or lame—suffering from both physical ailments and social ostracism—and to those who are captives or in prison, to encompass all persons who are oppressed. The good news of God's reign and God's blessing, furthermore, becomes incarnate in the concrete acts of care for "the poor" associated with Jesus' own ministry, and those by means of which people confess the Christ (Mark 10:21; 14:6–10; Luke 19:8–9). Those acts do not simply sustain the poor in their poverty, but instead result in substantive changes in people's circumstances, such that they enjoy the chance for a new beginning.[1]

Jubilee images for the proclamation of good news to the poor thus hold together what modern analysis and practice split apart. Most basically, the confession of Jesus as the Christ is portrayed as occurring in deeds of justice. Contemporary ecclesiastical disagreements over whether "faith" or "mission" should have priority in the church's agenda are thus circumvented in this confession that is recognized in one's care for the poor who are always with us (Mark 14:7//Matt. 26:11//John 12:8). Similarly, the academic theological debate over the relationship between Christology and ethics is resolved in their interconnection in the Jubilee images.

Second, human needs often experienced as competing for attention are brought together onto the single agenda of the Jubilee. That same common agenda provides a category by which to understand the various liberation theologies. Furthermore, the place of the Jubilee traditions in the Synoptic Gospels makes clear the centrality of concerns for liberation in the gospel. Far from being merely the political agenda of particular contemporary cultures and groups, these concerns emerge as fundamental to the proclamation of God's reign and to the collection of gospel portraits of Jesus as the Christ.

FORGIVENESS AND LIBERATION

("To proclaim release to captives, . . .
to set at liberty those who are oppressed")

Although theologians of liberation clearly recognize the importance of gospel imagery pointing to "good news to the poor," they seem not to be drawn to the theological motif of forgiveness, and for very good reason. From the mouths of various oppressors, it is heard as a word that would whitewash past abuses whose present consequences continue to be felt. To move too quickly to "forgiveness" in this fashion, without addressing the way patterns of oppression have become institutionalized, risks simply perpetuating the status quo. Before "forgiveness" can find its way back into the lexicon of liberation, it must be linked to justice.

The imagery of forgiveness present in the Jubilee traditions might address some of those concerns. "Forgiveness" in the Jubilee traditions is at heart a political word. The images by which forgiveness is presented in those traditions are of people set free from the de-humanizing effects of social role definitions (Luke 7:36–50; 19:1–10), from the stigma as well as the physical consequences of disease (Isa. 61:1–2; Mark 2:1–12), and from the vicious cycle of economic op-pression (Leviticus 25; Matt. 18:23–35). The traditions in which these images are found point to an actual change of circumstance for those who suffer, and thus to a change in the power relationship between oppressor and oppressed. Far from being an easy or cheap route of escape for the privileged, "forgiveness" becomes their "liberty" as well, whether that be the genuine liberty marked by acts of justice or the "liberty" of the consequences of business as usual (Jer. 34:17). As the satrap discovered (Matt. 18:23–35), if one opts to live with the pattern of forgiveness, that choice must govern those situations from which one benefits as well as those where one's own debt is insur-mountable.

The imagery of forgiveness developed in the Jubilee traditions sounds a note of caution to proponents of liberation as well for this "liberty" encompasses all of life. One form of oppression cannot be pitted against another, with each claiming priority. Rather, patterns of oppression and domination in all arenas of life are to be broken in this Jubilee of God's reign, or none is canceled. One is not punished for denying liberation to others, one simply chooses to live in a realm not of "liberty" but of indebtedness. The implication of the Jubilee tradi-tions is that such a choice against liberation finally denies the sov-ereignty of God. Like the message of "good news to the poor," "forgiveness" as an image of the Jubilee points to the political choice of standing with the oppressed, and in that choice confessing one's relationship to Christ and thus to God.

THE IMAGE OF GOD AS SOVEREIGN

("God has sent me to proclaim release")

The Jubilee is a royal decree of liberty. In its Gospel contexts, it is the decree of a sovereign God proclaimed by Jesus Christ the royal messenger. For some people, particularly people involved in libera-tion struggles, the very notion of a sovereign God jeopardizes the intent of liberation at the heart of the Jubilee. They conclude that such imagery introduces hierarchical patterns of divine omnipotence and human impotence that contradict the human urge toward liberation. They would maintain that these patterns not only suggest human dependence on an omnipotent God, but also lead to dependence on other persons who can claim convincingly to know what that God needs or requires of people. Advocates of liberation argue that the oppressed have internalized the powerless side of that dynamic to the point where they collude in their own oppression. At the same time, those with power draw on such images to support their claim to be spokespersons for the powerful God and representatives or guarantors of the order that is claimed to be consistent with God's will.

To speak of a sovereign God in biblical terms in general, however, is not to describe an omnipotent God and insignificant human beings. The primary vehicle by which God's sovereignty finds expression is God's initiation of covenants with humankind—covenants that are offered anew when human beings violate them. God's sovereignty thus finds its expression not in arbitrary expressions of power, but in relationship to human response. In Jubilee imagery in particular, where the accent is on the inaugural event of the new sovereign's reign and on the moment of a change of allegiance from the old order to the new, one can opt not to recognize the new reign and so to exclude oneself from it (Matt. 18:23–35).

The problem is thus not what the biblical traditions suggest about the sense in which God is sovereign. Rather, the problem lies in the human patterns of rule to which such language also refers, where sovereignty finds hierarchical and not covenantal expression. The problem is a serious one, for the language of sovereignty belongs to the concreteness of the Jubilee image, but human experience of that image impedes its being experienced in the liberating sense which it appears originally to have had. Poets and artists will perhaps need to find new images to express what Jubilee images and the Bible in general would say about the nature of God's sovereignty, until such time as people's experience of power incorporates justice and liberation.

Jubilee images of God as sovereign also suggest that to speak of God's sovereignty is to speak of the primacy of God over all creation. To say God is sovereign is to say that God, and not the various systems, ideologies, or other artifacts of human creation, has ultimate authority in one's life. Such institutions and systems of the created order are at once *necessary* to the organization and functioning of human life, and at the same time they *limit* people's response to God, neighbor, and self to familiar, predictable patterns. Even though these patterns are often oppressive in their consequences, they have the advantage of familiarity, and hence often seem more comfortable than more liberating but unfamiliar options. Furthermore, such systems, structures, and institutions require people's allegiance and obedience, since they represent the loci of social, economic, and political power. In the face of their power and control, which is unliberating, perhaps the image of God as the sovereign who comes declaring liberation can be reclaimed as an image particularly appropriate for the God of the poor and oppressed.

ESCHATOLOGY AND HUMAN RESPONSIBILITY

("To proclaim a year acceptable to God")

The perspective on time that is assumed in the Jubilee images found in the Synoptic Gospels is particularly difficult to grasp. Since those Jubilee images are associated with God's ultimate or eschatological reign, one time-related question is that of the relationship between God's reign and ongoing, chronological time. A second major question concerns the relationship of God's reign to human deeds of justice and liberation.

The first of these questions comes to focus in the fact that God's reign, which was proclaimed to be "at hand" so long ago, is still not in evidence in the institutions of society on which our human experience is based. How can the Jubilee message of Jesus continue to focus on the drama of a boundary moment of two thousand years' duration? What, indeed, can such a proclamation have to do with us any more? One answer is suggested in the previous paragraph, namely, that *whenever* human institutions and designs to enable business as usual are met by the proclamation of God's reign, we are always at that same boundary moment encountered first by Jesus' own hearers. In that boundary moment, human assumptions and pretensions hear the word of liberation that is required if God's own sovereignty is to be recognized.

The imagery of the Jubilee itself suggests an answer to the question concerning the relationship between God's reign and human deeds of justice. In both Hebrew Scriptures and the NT, the "release" of the Jubilee was, at most, seen as a once-in-a-lifetime event, whether according to the fifty-year cycle of Leviticus 25 or as the boundary moment of God's reign in Isaiah 61 and the NT. That suggests that *each generation* must take responsibility for responding to God's decree of liberty, and for doing justice, in its own circumstances and for its children. We cannot, from our human perspective, design structures and social organizations that will be eternally appropriate, and that will always and everywhere support concerns of justice and liberation. Such structures are appropriately referred to as *God's* realm, not a realm of human construction. But we are called by the imagery of the Jubilee to respond to that larger vision as it breaks into the institutions, systems, and world views that characterize life in our own time and place. Coming generations, in turn, will respond for themselves (if only we leave them a world in which to live), perhaps around issues and in ways that would astound us, even as our concerns and ways of acting seem foreign to the particular images of the biblical Jubilee traditions.

These Jubilee images, as images, transcend their own times and places of origin, and by their cultural and historical particularity they call us more fully into our own time and place. They challenge us to live with the rhythms of liberation and to proclaim good news to the poor at the particular points of pain, oppression, and alienation in our society and world. In doing that, we continue to confess Jesus as the Christ who is the herald of the Jubilee, messenger and enactor of liberation. That liberation, in turn, is our first encounter in all times and places with God's sovereign will for humankind.

Notes

CHAPTER 1. THE LANGUAGE OF ETHICS AND CHRISTOLOGY

1. P. Ricoeur, *The Symbolism of Evil,* trans. E. Buchanan (New York: Harper & Row, 1967), 10.

2. S. McFague, *Metaphorical Theology: Models of God in Religious Language* (Philadelphia: Fortress Press, 1982), 20.

3. See the discussion of principles of "expressive language" in P. Wheelwright, *The Burning Fountain: A Study in the Language of Symbolism* (Bloomington: Indiana Univ. Press, 1954), 60–75. See also the discussion of the role of such language in the NT in A. N. Wilder, *Early Christian Rhetoric: The Language of the Gospel* (Cambridge: Harvard Univ. Press, 1971), 118–28.

4. Ricoeur (*Symbolism of Evil,* 163–64) makes a similar point about the difference between myth and allegory. Allegory can be translated into direct discourse, then the allegory itself can be eliminated without any loss of meaning. Myth, on the other hand, "is autonomous and immediate; it means what it says."

5. M. Black, *Models and Metaphors: Studies in Language and Philosophy* (Ithaca: Cornell Univ. Press, 1962), 44–47. See also the discussion of metaphor in P. Trible, *God and the Rhetoric of Sexuality* (Philadelphia: Fortress Press, 1978), 17.

6. This is the perspective on parables presented in J. D. Crossan, *In Parables: The Challenge of the Historical Jesus* (New York: Harper & Row, 1973).

7. N. Perrin, *A Modern Pilgrimage in New Testament Christology* (Philadelphia: Fortress Press, 1974), 38.

8. P. Ricoeur, "The Language of Faith," trans. R. B. DeFord, *USQR* 28 (1973): 220–21. See also idem, *Symbolism of Evil,* 14–18.

9. Ricoeur, *Symbolism of Evil*, 19, 163–66; Perrin, *Modern Pilgrimage*, 38.

10. Wheelwright, *Burning Fountain*, 24.

11. P. Wheelwright, *Metaphor and Reality* (Bloomington: Indiana Univ. Press, 1962), 92.

12. Ibid., 105–8.

13. McFague, 55. In a similar vein, W. Brueggemann (*The Creative Word: Canon as a Model for Biblical Education* [Philadelphia: Fortress Press, 1982], 52) calls the writing prophets of Hebrew Scriptures speakers who "commit linguistic acts that assault the assumed world of the king." The primary task of these prophets is to nurture the poetic imagination, and only derivatively to influence action.

14. McFague, *Metaphorical Theology*, 62–64; S. (McFague) TeSelle, *Literature and the Christian Life* (New Haven, Conn.: Yale Univ. Press, 1966), 114; J. M. Gustafson, *Theology and Christian Ethics* (Philadelphia: Pilgrim Press, 1974), 151.

15. Brueggemann, *Creative Word*, 22–24.

16. McFague, *Metaphorical Theology*, 39.

17. Brueggemann, *Creative Word*, 53.

18. McFague, *Metaphorical Theology*, 56–57. See also Ricoeur, *Symbolism of Evil*, 351–52.

19. McFague, *Metaphorical Theology*, 65.

20. Choan-Seng Song, *Third-Eye Theology: Theology in Formation in Asian Settings* (Maryknoll, N.Y.: Orbis Books, 1979), 12–13.

21. E. Pagels (*The Gnostic Gospels* [New York: Random House, 1979]) suggests that precisely those criteria account for the harsh opposition to Gnosticism at a time of consolidation of polity and standardization of creeds in the early catholic church. For a discussion of the variety of expressions of the faith represented within the NT canon, see J. D. G. Dunn, *Unity and Diversity in the New Testament: An Inquiry Into the Character of Earliest Christianity* (Philadelphia: Westminster Press, 1977).

22. R. Radford Ruether, *To Change the World: Christology and Cultural Criticism* (New York: Crossroad, 1981), 3.

23. J. M. Gustafson, "The Place of Scripture in Christian Ethics: A Methodological Study," *Int* 24 (1970): 430–55; A. Verhey, "The Use of Scripture in Ethics," *RelSRev* 4 (1978): 28–39; S. Hauerwas, "The Moral Authority of Scripture," *Int* 23 (1980): 356–70; J. A. Sanders, "Torah and Christ," *Int* 29 (1975): 372–90.

24. Ruether, *To Change the World*, 5. See also L. Boff, *Jesus Christ Liberator: A Critical Christology for Our Time*, trans. P. Hughes (Maryknoll, N.Y.: Orbis Books, 1978), epilogue.

25. Ruether, *To Change the World*, 5.

26. In addition to Boff, see J. Sobrino, *Christology at the Crossroads: A Latin American Approach*, trans. J. Drury (Maryknoll, N.Y.: Orbis Books,

1978); G. Gutiérrez, *A Theology of Liberation: History, Politics and Salvation*, trans. C. Inda and J. Eagleson (Maryknoll, N.Y.: Orbis Books, 1973); A. A. Boesak, *A Farewell to Innocence: A Socio-Ethical Study on Black Theology and Black Power* (Maryknoll, N.Y.: Orbis Books, 1977); J. H. Cone, *A Black Theology of Liberation* (Philadelphia and New York: J. B. Lippincott, 1970); and idem, *God of the Oppressed* (New York: Seabury Press, 1975).

27. E. Schüssler Fiorenza, *In Memory of Her: A Feminist Theological Reconstruction of Christian Origins* (New York: Crossroad, 1983), 152.

28. The suggestion that Jesus functions as a parable of God is made by Crossan (*In Parables*, xiv), McFague (*Metaphorical Theology*, x, 18, 20, 48–50), J. Donahue ("Jesus as the Parable of God in the Gospel of Mark," *Int* 32 [1978]: 380–86), and L. Keck (*A Future for the Historical Jesus: The Place of Jesus in Preaching and Theology* [Philadelphia: Fortress Press, 1975], 244).

29. S. (McFague) TeSelle, *Speaking in Parables: A Study in Metaphor and Theology* (Philadelphia: Fortress Press, 1975), 46.

CHAPTER 2. JUBILEE TRADITIONS IN HEBREW SCRIPTURES

1. N. K. Gottwald, *The Tribes of Yahweh: A Sociology of the Religion of Liberated Israel 1250–1050 B.C.E.* (Maryknoll, N.Y.: Orbis Books, 1979), 615, 692–709. See also G. E. Mendenhall, *The Tenth Generation: The Origins of the Biblical Tradition* (Baltimore: Johns Hopkins Press, 1973), 1, 29–31.

2. The Covenant Code is a complex body of legislation. Far from speaking with a single voice, its laws support ethical perspectives that appear contradictory to one another. Despite some laws that appear to assume and support a stratified society (for example, Exod. 21:1–11, 22–32), P. D. Hanson finds at the heart of that code "a liberating dynamic which transcends the social vehicles within which it is carried. . . . From this unfolding dynamic emerged a challenge to injustice, inhumaneness, and idolatry wherever they occurred, even when they remained lodged at the heart of Israel's religious institutions" ("The Theological Significance of Contradiction within the Book of the Covenant," in *Canon and Authority: Essays in Old Testament Religion and Theology*, ed. G. W. Coats and B. O. Long [Philadelphia: Fortress Press, 1977], 129).

3. G. E. Mendenhall, "The Hebrew Conquest of Palestine," *BA* 25 (1962): 71; R. North, *Sociology of the Biblical Jubilee* (Rome: Pontifical Biblical Institute, 1954), 63; N. P. Lemche, "The 'Hebrew Slave,'" *VT* 25 (1975): 129–44.

4. F. Belo (*A Materialist Reading of the Gospel of Mark*, trans. M. J. O'Connell [Maryknoll, N.Y.: Orbis Books, 1981], 37–59) draws on insights from Marxist social analysis to discover that it is in fact the system regulating

indebtedness that is at the heart of Israelite legal codes and of various reform movements within Israel. He concludes that in the symbolic order of ancient Israel, concerns about cultic purity were often expressed in the economic language of "debts" and "debtors," and that indeed the cultic and economic systems were intertwined. Given this situation, it would seem only reasonable that provisions for the canceling of debts in both sabbath and Jubilee years would be restricted to those within the religious community of Israel.

5. For a discussion of the content and development of the *prôzbûl*, see J. Neusner, *The Rabbinic Traditions About the Pharisees Before 70*, 3 vols. (Leiden: E. J. Brill, 1971), 1: 217–23.

6. J. Lewy, "The Biblical Institution of *Dĕrôr* in the Light of Akkadian Documents," *Eretz-Israel* 5 (1958): 21-31.

7. R. V. Bergren, *The Prophets and the Law*, HUC Monograph 4 (New York: Ktav Publ., 1974), 68–74; W. L. Holladay, "A Fresh Look at 'Source B' and 'Source C' in Jeremiah," *VT* 25 (1975): 394–412; H. Weippert, *Die Prosareden des Jeremiabuches* (New York and Berlin: Walter de Gruyter, 1973), 86–106.

8. A. Jirku, "Das israelitische Jobeljahr," in *Von Jerusalem nach Ugarit: Gesammelte Schriften* (Graz: Akademische Druck- und Verlaganstalt, 1966), 321, 326–28; North, *Sociology of Biblical Jubilee,* 191–212; M. Noth, *Leviticus,* trans. J. E. Anderson (Philadelphia: Westminster Press, 1965), 184–85.

9. North, *Sociology of Biblical Jubilee,* 206–11. Two traditions concerning the reallocation of the land after the exile (Ezek. 47:13—48:29 and 48:30–35) disagree on the actual division of the real estate, but agree in interpreting the distribution of the land as a manifestation of God's abiding presence. See R. W. Klein, *Israel in Exile: A Theological Interpretation* (Philadelphia: Fortress Press, 1979), 90–96.

10. P. D. Hanson, *The Dawn of Apocalyptic: The Historical and Sociological Roots of Jewish Apocalyptic Eschatology,* rev. ed. (Philadelphia: Fortress Press, 1979), 71–77. See also E. Achtemeier, *The Community and Message of Isaiah 56—66* (Minneapolis: Augsburg Publ. House, 1982).

11. Hanson, *Dawn of Apocalyptic,* 44.

12. Ibid., 72–76.

13. See, for example, Isa. 42:6–7; 49:8–13; 58:1–14, and Isa. 29:17–21 and 35:1–10 (which may also come from the hand of Second Isaiah). W. Brueggemann ("Unity and Dynamic in the Isaiah Tradition," *JSOT* 29 [1984]: 98–102) suggests that the oracles of Third Isaiah move beyond those of Second Isaiah precisely in that while the earlier oracles are "about the public embrace of pain as the way to return to the old stories" of Israel's faith, the later ones "*release social imagination*" (italics his).

14. The example at issue is a cuneiform inscription telling of Sargon's liberation of Dur Yakin. See the discussion in S. Paul, "Deutero-Isaiah and Cuneiform Royal Inscriptions," *JAOS* 88 (1968): 180–86.

15. F. M. Cross, *Canaanite Myth and Hebrew Epic: Essays in the History of the Religion of Israel* (Cambridge: Harvard Univ. Press, 1973), 186–90.

16. See the discussion of the identity of the speaker in Isaiah 61 in W. Zimmerli, "Das 'Gnadenjahr des Herrn'," in *Archaeologie und Altes Testament,* ed. A. Kuschke and E. Kutsch (Tübingen: J. C. B. Mohr [Paul Siebeck] 1970), 321–23.

17. S. Mowinckel, *He That Cometh,* trans. G. W. Anderson (Nashville: Abingdon Press, 1954), 338.

18. The literature of late Second Temple Judaism supports a reading of this passage that understands it as pointing to God's approaching eschatological reign. Of the rabbinic traditions in which Isa. 61:1–2 is prominent, at least two which appear to stem from this early period, *Targum Pseudo-Jonathan* and *Midrash 'Ekah* to 3:50 (73a), relate this passage to the awaited eschaton. (See J. A. Sanders, "From Isaiah 61 to Luke 4," in *Christianity, Judaism and Other Greco-Roman Cults: Studies for Morton Smith at Sixty,* ed. J. Neusner, 4 vols. [Leiden: E. J. Brill, 1975], 1: 87–88.) In the *Melchizedek* scroll from Cave 11 at Qumran, Leviticus 25, Deuteronomy 15, and Isaiah 52 and 61 are interwoven in an intricate midrash depicting an eschatological Jubilee proclamation. "Melchizedek" is depicted in this midrash as both a heavenly figure involved in the judgment and redemption associated with the end time and an earthly herald of salvation. Thus the figure of Melchizedek, while not one of the messiahs expected by the Qumran community, combines a heavenly identity or origin and an earthly function. (See J. A. Sanders, "The Old Testament in 11 Q *Melchizedek,*" *JANESCU* 5: *Theodor H. Gaster Festschrift* [1973]: 373–82; J. T. Milik, "Milkî-ṣedeq et Milkî-reša' dans les anciens écrits juifs et chrétiens," *JJS* 23 [1972]: 95–144; M. de Jonge and A. S. van der Woude, "11 Q *Melchizedek* and the New Testament," *NTS* 12 [1965–66]: 301–26.)

CHAPTER 3. JESUS AS HERALD OF LIBERATION

1. The fact that much of their discussion is based on just such alleged references to Leviticus 25, along with their failure to engage in careful literary and historical criticism of those pericopes to which they refer, make the provocative works of A. Trocmé (*Jésus-Christ et la revolution non-violente* [Geneva: Labor et Fides, 1961]) and J. H. Yoder (*The Politics of Jesus* [Grand Rapids: Wm. B. Eerdmans, 1972]) less than convincing. Two additional discussions of Jubilee traditions in the NT about which similar questions might be raised, but which are significant in the theological points they make, are L. M. Russell, *Growth in Partnership* (Philadelphia: Westminster Press, 1981), 112–18 and 178–79, and J. C. Hoekendijk, "Mission—A Celebration of Freedom," *USQR* 21 (1966): 135–43.

2. The prominence of the account of the rejection of Jesus at Nazareth,

with its quotation of Isa. 61:1–2, in the Gospel of Luke has prompted several recent studies on the role of Jubilee traditions in Lukan redaction. The more cautious of these discuss the quotation from Isaiah without emphasizing its character as a Jubilee text. (See, for example, Sanders, "From Isaiah 61 to Luke 4," 75–106; R. C. Tannehill, "The Mission of Jesus according to Luke iv. 16–30," in *Jesus in Nazareth*, ed. E. Grässer et al. [New York and Berlin: Walter de Gruyter, 1972], 51–75; L. C. Crockett, "The Old Testament in the Gospel of Luke" [Ph.D. diss., Brown University, 1966]; D. H. Hill, "The Rejection of Jesus at Nazareth [Luke iv 16–30]," *NovT* 13 [1971]: 161–80; J. Elias, "The Beginning of Jesus' Ministry in the Gospel of Luke" [Ph.D. diss., Toronto School of Theology, 1978].) R. B. Sloan, Jr., does point to the significance of the Jubilee in countering the conclusion of H. Conzelmann that a major Lukan concern was to de-emphasize the eschatological urgency of the Gospel and to set it in the context of ongoing history. Sloan maintains that Luke views the Jubilee as an eschatological metaphor and presents his portrait of Jesus in terms of that metaphor (*The Favorable Year of the Lord: A Study of Jubilary Theology in the Gospel of Luke* [Austin: Schola, 1977]). In a methodologically ambiguous study that appears to assume the historical accuracy of Luke's portrayal of Jesus, D. Blosser looks at the place of Jubilee traditions in Luke's Gospel, but draws conclusions about Jesus' own ethical agenda ("Jesus and Jubilee, Luke 4:16–30: The Year of Jubilee and Its Significance in Luke" [Ph.D. diss., St. Andrews University, 1979]). J. Massyngbaerde Ford's redaction-critical study of Luke focusing on the issue of nonviolence (*My Enemy Is My Guest: Jesus and Violence in Luke* [Maryknoll, N.Y.: Orbis Books, 1984], 56–59) recognizes the Jubilee roots of the Nazareth pericope. The author contrasts Luke's treatment of those traditions with the martial imagery associated with them in 11QMelch. A major point in her argument is that Jesus was focusing on a particular calendar for his Jubilee proclamation, in keeping with the cyclical Jubilee pattern of Leviticus 25.

3. That is the conclusion drawn by J. A. Fitzmyer (*The Gospel According to Luke I–IX* [Garden City, N.Y.: Doubleday & Co., 1981], 529).

4. J. Jeremias, *Jesus' Promise to the Nations*, trans. S. H. Hooke (Philadelphia: Fortress Press, 1982; London: SCM Press, 1958), 44–46.

5. Both Jeremias (ibid.) and Sanders ("From Isaiah 61 to Luke 4," 96–99) suggest that Luke's portrayal of Jesus as omitting the last half of v. 2 is important for the point Luke is making. Sanders links that point to the prophetic hermeneutic that he sees at work in the passage, and to the specific hermeneutic device of the wordplay on the "acceptable year."

6. The work of A. Guilding (*The Fourth Gospel and Jewish Worship* [Oxford: At the Clarendon Press, 1960]), in which she claims to present evidence for the use in Jesus' time of a three-year lectionary cycle including both Torah and Prophets, has been refuted by most scholars. On this point, see the review of her book by R. E. Brown (*CBQ* 22 [1960]: 459–61) and the

following studies: P. Billerbeck, "Ein Synagogengottesdienst in Jesu Tagen," *ZNW* 55 (1964): 155; Hill, "Rejection of Jesus," 172–74; W. Eltester, "Israel im lukanischen Werk und die Nazarethperikope," in *Jesus in Nazareth,* ed. Grässer et al., 136; L. Morris, *The New Testament and the Jewish Lectionaries* (London: Tyndale Press, 1964), 15–21; L. C. Crockett, "Luke iv.16–30 and the Jewish Lectionary: A Word of Caution," *JJS* 17 (1966): 26–44; C. Perrot, *La Lecture de la Bible dans la Synagogue: les anciennes lectures palestiniennes du Shabbat et des fêtes* (Hildesheim: H. A. Gerstenberg, 1973), 139–40; Fitzmyer, *Gospel According to Luke I–IX,* 531. Several scholars have suggested that the incorporation of the quotation from Isaiah has its roots in exegetical, homiletical, or liturgical traditions that may have been known to Jesus. The evidence supporting such suggestions, however, is also inconclusive, since little is known about either synagogue worship in the late Second Temple period or worship in the early church (in contrast to such sectarian groups as the community at Qumran, about whose liturgical practice a great deal is known). See, for example, Crockett, "Luke iv.16–30," 45–46 nn. 84, 85; A. Finkel, *The Pharisees and the Teacher of Nazareth,* AGJU 4 (Leiden: E. J. Brill, 1964), 155–68, and idem, "Jesus' Sermon at Nazareth (Luke 4, 16–30)," in *Abraham Unser Vater: Juden und Christen im Gespräch über die Bibel: Festschrift für Otto Michel,* ed. O. Betz et al. (Leiden: E. J. Brill, 1963), 111–15; Hill, "Rejection of Jesus," 176–80; Perrot, *La Lecture de la Bible,* 195–204; Sanders, "From Isaiah 61 to Luke 4," 92–104.

7. At issue is whether Jesus "unrolled" (*anaptyxas*) or "opened" (*anoixas*) the *biblion*. The third edition of *UBSGNT* gives *anaptyxas* a "C" rating, indicating considerable doubt whether it or *anoixas* is the preferable reading. That rating seems appropriate on the basis of both external and internal evidence. The weight of manuscripts seems fairly evenly distributed between the two readings. Furthermore, on the basis of internal evidence neither reading is clearly the stronger. If what is described is understood to be a book, *anoixas* seems the preferable verb. One can see how an original reading of *anaptyxas* might thus have been corrected by a later copyist. On the other hand, since Luke 4:20 describes Jesus' action as "rolling up" (*ptyxas*) the book or scroll, with no variant reading suggested at that point, one can also see how an original reading of *anoixas* might have been changed to mirror this action. Unless one resolves the several ambiguities presented by the text in terms of a prior assumption that Jesus was handed a scroll already preset to the correct text, which he therefore had simply to open in order to read, the setting itself does not prove or disprove the lectionary hypothesis.

8. The Beatitudes found in the Sermons on the Mount and on the Plain (Matt. 5:3–6/ /Luke 6:20–22), on the other hand, appear to be a meditation on the content of Isa. 61:1–2.

9. The verb *martureō* occurs in Luke only at 4:22. The five occurrences of the verb with the dative case in Acts (10:43; 13:22; 14:3; 15:8; 22:5) all refer

to a positive witness in favor of the object, or, in the last instance, neutral witness to the accuracy of a point. Of the twenty-four occurrences of the verb *thaumazō* in the Synoptic Gospels, thirteen are in Luke. Five more are found in Acts. Of all of those examples, only two indicate a clearly negative response (Luke 11:38; 20:26), and Acts 4:13 is ambiguous. The rest all point to the sort of wonder and awe that suggests that the subjects were positively impressed by what they witnessed (Luke 1:21, 63; 2:18, 33; 7:9; 8:25; 9:43; 11:14; 24:41; Acts 2:7; 3:12; 7:31). The weight of the evidence is therefore in favor of interpreting the people's response in Luke 4:22 in a positive light, contrary to the arguments of Jeremias (*Jesus' Promise to Nations*, 44–46) and B. Violet ("Zum rechten Verständnis der Nazareth-Perikope Lc 4:16–30," *ZNW* 37 [1938]: 251–71).

10. This point is made also by Tannehill, "Mission of Jesus," 53. It is confirmed in Luke 2:48–49, where Luke portrays Mary as speaking of Joseph as Jesus' father, and Jesus as responding that God is "my father."

11. The meaning of the future tense of the verb *ereite* is problematic if one does not understand it in the conversational sense suggested. Perhaps it might be considered as a "gnomic future," expressing "that which is to be expected under certain circumstances" (BDF 178.349), even though BDF does not list this as an example of that usage. H. Flender (*St. Luke: Theologian of Redemptive History*, trans. R. H. Fuller and I. Fuller [Philadelphia: Fortress Press, 1967], 156–57) understands this verse to mirror the Markan pericope in suggesting that the hostility that Jesus encountered in Nazareth was related to his performing few if any miracles there. Hill ("Rejection of Jesus," 166–67), Tannehill ("Mission of Jesus," 54–58), Fitzmyer (*Gospel According to Luke I–IX*, 526), and P. D. Miller, Jr. ("Luke 4:16–21," *Int* 29 [1975]: 418) suggest that this verse is a Lukan composition, in which he is drawing a contrast between the event at Nazareth and the ones at Capernaum which he describes later (4:31–41), but which he knows from his source have occurred prior to the episode at Nazareth.

12. Verse 24 begins with a reintroduction of the speaker in the middle of a speech. In this case, however, that reintroduction need not indicate an editorial seam as it often does. Since the speaker has been quoting what others will say, the repetition of the verb makes clear that it is Jesus himself who is responding in what follows. Indeed, the response is introduced with the solemn phrase, "Amen, I say to you," which is used in Luke to underline a particularly important or summary statement attributed to Jesus (4:24; 12:37; 18:17; 21:32; 23:43). The proverb quoted in that verse is closer to the forms in which it is found in *Gos. Thom.* 31 and *P. Oxy.* I.6 than to those in Mark 6:4a, Matt. 13:57b, or John 4:44. The literary relationship between Luke's version and any of these others is impossible to discern. However, it is reasonable to assume that several forms of the proverb may have circulated independently. Luke's version appears to incorporate a subtle pun on the concluding word of the quotation from Isaiah (*dektos*). Whether that pun was

deliberately inserted is impossible to say. Hill ("Rejection of Jesus," 167), Tannehill ("Mission of Jesus," 59), Fitzmyer (*Gospel According to Luke I–IX,* 528), and Sanders ("From Isaiah 61 to Luke 4," 98–99) all conclude that the pun is central to Luke's point. In favor of that conclusion is the fact that it is a relatively rare word, occurring only three times in the NT outside of these two verses (Acts 10:35; 2 Cor. 6:2; Phil. 4:18). The two occurrences in this pericope are at some distance from each other, however, so whether Luke would have expected it to have caught the hearer's or reader's attention is difficult to know. The point of 4:24 remains the same, though, whether or not the link to 4:19 is recognized.

13. Fitzmyer, *Gospel According to Luke I–IX,* 537; Tannehill, "Mission of Jesus," 59–62; Hill, "Rejection of Jesus," 170; H. Anderson, "Broadening Horizons: The Rejection at Nazareth Pericope of Luke 4:16–30 in Light of Recent Critical Trends," *Int* 18 (1964): 266–72; J. M. Creed, *The Gospel According to St. Luke* (London: Macmillan & Co., 1930), 66; E. E. Ellis, *The Gospel of Luke* (London: Thomas Nelson & Sons, 1966), 98. According to this argument, since these verses deal with the contrast between Israel and the Gentiles, they are of a totally different order from the proverb in 4:23, which is understood to be playing up a supposed rivalry between the two villages. Seen in that light, the Elijah and Elisha references would be incongruous with the ministry of Jesus, and would be part of Luke's or the early church's redaction. A variation on this argument suggests that the Elijah and Elisha traditions are not stories of God's or the prophet's rejection of Israel in favor of the Gentiles. Rather, each story tells of the prophet being given a special responsibility of bringing help or blessing to a Gentile, which has the result that Israelites and Gentiles both benefit. These stories thus would provide a vehicle by which Luke can develop an issue of great importance to his theology, namely, the issue of Jewish-Gentile relations or even reconciliation. For the latter argument, see L. C. Crockett, "Luke 4:25–27 and Jewish-Gentile Relations in Luke-Acts," *JBL* 88 (1969): 177–83.

14. The prominence of themes found in this sermon elsewhere in Luke and in summary statements in Acts argues for this being a programmatic sermon. D. Tiede (*Prophecy and History in Luke-Acts* [Philadelphia: Fortress Press, 1980], 19–63) argues that rejection is an organizing theme of Luke's writings, which would further substantiate the suggestion that this pericope is virtually a gospel-in-miniature.

15. The details of Schürmann's argument are developed in the course of his discussion of the pericope in his commentary (*Das Lukasevangelium: Erster Teil* [Freiburg: Herder, 1969]). Although Fitzmyer (*Gospel According to Luke I–IX,* 527) dismisses the argument as "tenuous," both the particular details and their cumulative effect demand that Schürmann's argument be taken seriously. He begins by pointing out that the summary statement in Luke 4:14–15 is not a reworking of Mark 1:14–15, but finds its origins in Q, on which Matthew and Luke both drew (*Das Lukasevangelium,* 223–24). He

points to Matthew's and Luke's unusual spelling of *Nazara* as added evidence of their common source, since both elsewhere spell the name *Nazaret* or *Nazareth* (Matt. 2:23; 21:11; Luke 1:26; 2:4, 38, 51; Acts 10:38). Having identified details concerning the synagogue service, the non-Lukan use of the word *biblion* (instead of *biblios*) to refer to a book from Hebrew Scriptures, and several Semitisms, Schürmann concludes that these verses also have their origin in a pre-Lukan, possibly a Palestinian, context. Furthermore, because they point to a pre-Lukan tradition, it is probable that the Isaiah reference in Luke 4:18–19 (though not in its present Greek form) was also a part of that source. As added support for that conclusion, Schürmann calls attention to the fact that the same text from Isaiah is also found in two other Q texts, namely, Luke 7:22 and 6:20–22 and their Matthean parallels. He then rejects the notion that Luke 4:22–23 is Luke's independent reworking of Mark 6:3, first because there is no evidence of other places where Luke inserted material occurring later in Mark's sequence into an earlier portion of Q. Second, it is unlikely that Luke would have altered the word "astonished" *(exeplēssonto)* from Mark 6:2 if he were working from Mark, since that word would have made a smoother transition between 4:22 and 23. Finally, Schürmann points to "son of Joseph" both as reflecting a possible Aramaism and as reflecting traditional language found also in John 6:42. He cites the "proverb" in Luke 4:23a as evidence of a Palestinian language background for that verse, and points out also that the reference to a physician and to healing correspond to the phrase of Isa. 61:1 omitted in Luke (ibid., 227–37). Schürmann admits that Luke 4:24 may be seen as a logical intrusion between 4:23 and 25, but he says that it is not necessary to interpret it as such, since it also appears that Luke did not get the "amen" saying from Mark, and that it too may well have been in the other source, perhaps already combined with 4:23 and 25. He points to the fact that the Gentile mission is not a theme found elsewhere in Luke prior to 24:47, and that Luke does not use the masculine form of the word "famine" *(limos)* elsewhere in his writings, to substantiate his assertion that 4:25–27 is not an independent Lukan creation, and probably does not owe its presence to a Lukan insertion. Indeed, Schürmann notes that those verses share the universalizing tendency that he says is characteristic of Q. Finally, 4:28–30 is not found in Mark. It does contain what Schürmann identifies as a Semitism (4:29—"on which the city was built"). With their connection to the theme of false prophecy, these verses seem to provide a fitting conclusion to the account with its accent on prophecy. Schürmann thus concludes that Luke 4:16–30 is not a Lukan composition, but rather an alternate strand of the tradition of Jesus' experience at Nazareth (ibid., 238–41). Concerning the point in the Gospel narrative where the rejection pericope is presented, Schürmann (228) cites not only the coherence of Luke 4:14–15 with the pericope which follows, but also the resemblance between Matt. 9:26 and Luke 4:14b as a reason why one should consider the possibility that Luke has placed this pericope in its correct order according to Q. He notes that Luke 4:14b immediately precedes the account of the rejection pericope, as does the story of the healing of Jairus's daughter in the Markan chronology. Matthew 9:26, in turn, concludes Matthew's version of the story of Jairus's daughter. Schürmann concludes, therefore, that Luke 4:14–15 must also be from Q, and that that Q text immediately preceded the rejection pericope, as it still does in Luke. Schürmann's argument on this point is weak for two reasons. First, in Matthew's order the rejection pericope does not follow immediately after the healing of Jairus's daughter, but in fact is separated from it by several chapters. To conclude that Matthew deliberately inserted a phrase from Q at a point in the Markan order that Matthew then does not follow seems to be unwarranted. Had Matthew placed the rejection pericope immediately after 9:26, Schürmann's argument would have been stronger. Furthermore, while there are similarities between Luke 4:14b and Matt. 9:26, the two are neither identical nor so remarkable as to require that they be drawn from a common source and not composed independently.

16. Sanders, "From Isaiah 61 to Luke 4," 94–95.

17. Ibid., 96–98.

18. See, for example, Matt. 9:3/ /Mark 2:6–7/ /Luke 5:21; Matt. 9:11–13/ / Mark 2:16–17/ /Luke 5:30–32; Matt. 12:9–14/ /Mark 3:1–6/ /Luke 6:6–11.

CHAPTER 4. JUBILEE IMAGES: GOOD NEWS TO THE POOR

1. G. Friedrich, "euaggelizomai, euaggelion, proeuaggelizomai, euaggelistēs," *TDNT* 2: 707–13. See, for example, 1 Sam. 31:9; 2 Sam. 4:10, 18, 19, 27(26), 31; 1 Kings 1:42; 1 Chron. 10:9; Pss. 39(40):9; 67:11(68:12); 95(96):2; Isa. 40:9; 52:7; 60:6; Jer. 20:15; Nahum 1:14(2:1). Both the verb and the noun appear most frequently in summary statements about Jesus' significance, which are discussed in chapter 6. The verb is not found in Mark, and occurs only once in Matthew (11:5), but is found ten times in Luke and fifteen times in Acts. It is used most often in the absolute sense, with no direct object (Luke 1:19; 3:18; 4:18; 7:22; 9:6; 20:1; Acts 8:25, 40; 14:7, 15, 21; 16:10). When it has a direct object, in Luke it is usually "realm" or "reign" (4:43; 8:1; 16:16) and in Acts it is Jesus (5:42; 8:35; 11:20; 17:18). In Acts 8:12, both objects are present. The noun, on the other hand, is not found in Luke and appears only twice in Acts, but it occurs four times in Matthew and seven times in Mark (plus once in the so-called longer ending). It is used in an absolute sense in Matt. 26:13; Mark 1:15; 8:35; 13:10; 14:9; 16:15; Acts 15:7. It is used with "realm" in Matt. 4:23; 9:35; 24:14, and with "Christ" or "God" in Mark 1:1, 14; Acts 20:24.

2. D. Flusser, "Blessed Are the Poor in Spirit," *IEJ* 10 (1960): 1–13.

3. Grammatically this sense is captured by the negative of the present imperative, which indicates that something already taking place is to stop (Mark 5:36; 6:50; Luke 5:10; 8:50, 52; John 5:45; 20:17; James 1:7).

4. In the *Gospel of Thomas* the excuses are elaborately developed, as if to highlight the dangers of material cares that distract one from the pursuit of *gnōsis*. In Matthew the point of view of the host is given in great detail, and the core parable has been developed into a tale involving a king, a wedding feast, murdering guests, marauding armies, and finally a banquet hall overflowing with people. How to interpret that parable and the attached parable about the improperly attired guest continues to be controversial. Most scholars conclude that the elaborate detail points to an allegory whose point of reference is the course of salvation history. See E. Linnemann, *Jesus of the Parables: Introduction and Exposition,* trans. J. Sturdy from the 3d German ed. (New York: Harper & Row, 1966), 88–97, 158–68 (published also as *Parables of Jesus: Introduction and Exposition* [London: SPCK, 1966], 88–97, 158–68); J. Jeremias, *The Parables of Jesus,* rev. ed., trans. S. H. Hooke from the 6th German ed. (New York: Charles Scribners' Sons), 176–80; Crossan, *In Parables,* 70–73; D. O. Via, Jr., *The Parables: Their Literary and Existential Dimension* (Philadelphia: Fortress Press, 1967), 128–32.

5. Interpreters have usually assumed that the double sending of the servant is a detail supplied by Luke, but they have understood that sending as an allegorical reference to the Jewish and Gentile missions. Following this interpretation, the first group of guests brought in would refer to the outcasts in Israel to whom Jesus' own message was directed, and the second group (from outside the "city") would be a later addition by Luke to refer to the Gentile mission of the church.

6. The following comparison is drawn from J. A. Sanders, "The Ethic of Election in Luke's Great Banquet Parable," in *Essays in Old Testament Ethics: J. Philip Hyatt in Memoriam,* ed. J. L. Crenshaw and J. T. Willis (New York: Ktav Publ., 1974), 262:

Lev. 21:17–23	1QSa ii 5–22	1QM vii 4–6
blind	afflicted in flesh	(women and boys)
lame	crushed feet or hands	lame
mutilated face	lame	blind
limb too long	blind	halt
injured foot or hand	deaf	permanent defect in
dwarf	defective eyesight	the flesh
defective eyesight	senility	impurity of the flesh
itching disease	(i 19–20—the simple)	impure sexual organs
scabs		
crushed testicles		
any blemish		

7. The source of the banquet parable is Q, and that of the parables of the Prodigal (15:11–32) and of the Rich Man and Lazarus (16:19–31) is L.

8. The pattern of this story is quite similar to the incident of the lawyer's question (Luke 10:25–28) and to the exchange between Jesus and a scribe

presented in Matt. 22:34–40//Mark 12:28–31. In each case, a question evokes a response from Jesus that is in some way an amplification or interpretation of the law.

9. R. Bultmann (*The History of the Synoptic Tradition*, trans. J. Marsh from the 2d German ed., with corrections and additions from the 1962 Supplement [New York: Harper & Row, 1968], 34) suggests that Luke 19:1–10 is an imaginative expansion by Luke of the Markan story recorded earlier, into which Zacchaeus's promise (v. 8) and the saying in v. 10 were incorporated. See also Massyngbaerde Ford, *My Enemy Is My Guest*, 76.

10. J. R. Donahue ("Tax Collectors and Sinners: An Attempt at Identification," *CBQ* 33 [1971]: 39–61) has concluded that in Jesus' day the *telōnai* were properly considered toll collectors, and would have been responsible for collecting such things as sales and customs duties and taxes on transport. They would have been considered sinners because of their reputed dishonesty. By the time of the Gospel writers, the tax-gathering system would have come more closely under Roman control, and those who participated in it would have been seen as traitors who had "made themselves Gentiles" in their collaboration with Rome.

11. The vocative *kyrie*, which occurs later in the verse, does not necessarily carry the meaning of a title, but may be seem as simply a respectful address. For Luke it clearly carried both meanings, as a play on words that readers in the early church would surely understand.

12. Whatever the specific nature of the revenues he collected, Zacchaeus would have been suspected of having lined his pockets by setting excessive rates. His response, however, is not a confession of guilt, for he says, "*if* I have defrauded anyone . . ." Nonetheless, his promise to give away half of his goods, and to restore four times any amount of which he may have defrauded anyone, matches the most stringent requirements of the law, as if he has deliberately stolen and destroyed another's property (Exod. 22:1; 2 Sam. 12:6; Prov. 6:31).

13. A word needs to be said about the parable of the Rich Man and Lazarus and the theme of "good news to the poor." That parable reflects a theme common to folk tales of many traditions, namely, the reversal of fortunes in the afterlife. Furthermore, the rich man's suffering is ascribed to his having failed to show compassion to Lazarus, and he is said to want to warn his brothers to change their behavior at precisely that point. On the surface, then, this parable does appear to be another example of the message of "good news to the poor." On closer examination, however, that appears not to be the case. First, the accent in the parable is on one's fate following death, whereas other passages dealing with the message of good news to the poor address life in this world. Second, the passage speaks less to the needs of the poor than to the self-interest of the rich. Third, the parable affirms the continuing validity of the law, which Luke views as superseded by the proclamation of God's reign (16:16–17). Even though it is true that one of the

illustrations of the laws that continue to be valid does have to do with the relationship between rich and poor, this parable should not be included among the texts that elaborate the theme of "good news to the poor" in the context of the proclamation of God's reign.

14. The many critical issues posed by the various anointing stories, as well as the collection of scholarly studies on the subject, are helpfully reviewed in R. Holst, "The One Anointing of Jesus: Another Application of the Form-Critical Method," *JBL* 95 (1976): 435–46.

15. Both E. E. Platt ("The Ministry of Mary of Bethany," *TToday* 34 [1977]: 29–39) and J. K. Elliott ("The Anointing of Jesus," *ExpTim* 85 [1974]: 105–7) make the point that the anointing of Jesus' head recalls the ritual of consecration of a sovereign. This powerful political meaning of the episode is muted in Mark's version, they conclude, both in the emphasis on the woman's love in contrast with the opposition of Judas and the leaders of the Jews, and in the attempt to relieve the church's embarrassment at having failed to carry out the proper anointing of Jesus' body. In Luke 7:36–50 and John 12:1–8, a woman is described as anointing Jesus' feet and not his head, so the political gesture there becomes more like the gesture of hospitality common in first-century Palestine, except that the woman is said to use costly ointment instead of oil. It is clear, however, that even if the political dimension of the anointing is present, none of the Gospel writers has capitalized on it.

CHAPTER 5. JUBILEE IMAGES: "RELEASE" OR "FORGIVENESS"

1. R. Bultmann, "aphiēmi, aphesis; pariēmi, paresis," *TDNT* 1:509–10. *Aphiēmi* is used to translate such verbs as *kpr* ("pacify," "make propitiation," "cover over," or "atone"), *nś'* ("lift," "carry," "take," "take away," "be responsible for," "suffer," "sustain," "support," "permit," "bear with," "forgive"), and *slḥ* ("forgive," "pardon"). It should be noted that in the literature of Qumran the sense of forgiveness captured by the Greek terms is rare, for in that community sin was understood primarily as defilement or impurity, and forgiveness was talked about in metaphors of cleansing. (H. Ringgren, *The Faith of Qumran: Theology of the Dead Sea Scrolls,* trans. E. T. Sander [Philadelphia: Fortress Press, 1963]: 121–23.) In nascent rabbinic Judaism, the dual thrust of the language of forgiveness, including both cultic and covenantal expressions, was sustained. As J. Milgrom and A. Unterman observe ("Forgiveness," *EncJud* 6: cols. 1433–37), in Judaism one of the primary designations of God is in the role of forgiver (for example, Exod. 34:7; Num. 14:18; Hosea 14:3; Micah 7:18; Ps. 32:5). Much of the Jewish vocabulary for forgiveness was drawn from cultic terminology of cleansing, but even in the cultic setting forgiveness was recognized as granted by God and not by the priest. Gradually the ritual meaning of forgiveness was subsumed under the ethical meaning, in which forgiveness was seen as being

granted by God after a person's repentance (including both confession of the wrong that had been committed and resolution to depart from evil). That process was expressed in the verb *šûb*, which developed into the rabbinic doctrine of *tešûbah*, which implies that the person is endowed by God with the power of turning, thus activating God's concern and forgiveness. The rabbis' confidence of this fact was based on the covenant relationship, and on their perception of God as the parent who loves the children. Furthermore, they trusted God's acceptance of a mediator or intercessor, God's promise that Israel will exist forever, and the fact that God's own honor is at stake in the world because of the covenant. They understood that the human role in the process is to be ready to forgive an injurer and to pray for God's forgiveness for the sinner. There are two reasons why a person would be forgiving: self-interest, in that one can thereby earn God's favor; and the imitation of God. These two reasons are combined in a saying attributed to Rabbi Nahman: "Imitate God by being compassionate and forgiving. God will in turn have compassion on you and pardon your offenses."

2. Although Luke is aware of two other expressions for forgiveness (*apoluō* in 6:37 and *charizomai* in 7:42–43), and all three evangelists show awareness of situations in which Jewish practice required ritual purification (Matt. 23:25–26//Mark 7:19; Acts 10:15; 11:9), *aphiēmi* and *aphesis* are by far the most common words for forgiveness in the NT. The noun occurs in Matt. 26:28; Mark 1:4; 3:29; Luke 1:77; 4:18; 24:47; Acts 2:38; 5:31; 10:43; 13:28; 26:18; Eph. 1:7; Heb. 9:22; 10:18. The verb occurs in Matt. 6:12//Luke 11:4; Matt. 6:14–15//Mark 11:25–26; Matt. 9:2, 5, 6//Mark 2:5, 7, 9–10//Luke 5:20, 21, 23, 24; Matt. 12:32//Mark 3:28//Luke 12:10 [implied]; Matt. 18:27, 32; Luke 7:47–49; John 20:23; Acts 8:22; James 5:15; 1 John 1:9; 2:12. See also the discussion of *aphesis* in Miller, "Luke 4:16–21," 419–20.

3. This conclusion is drawn by Holst ("One Anointing of Jesus," 443).

4. This position is represented by Schürmann (Das Lukasevangelium, 441–42), who concludes that the two accounts were combined in the pre-Lukan tradition. A similar proposal, though developed in greater detail, is presented by R. E. Brown (*The Gospel According to John* [Garden City, N.Y.: Doubleday & Co., 1966], 450–52). He concludes that accounts of two different kinds of incidents lie behind the anointing stories. First, there is a story set in Galilee at the home of a Pharisee, in which a woman intrudes on a dinner party, weeps profusely at Jesus' feet, and wipes them with her unbound hair. The story then focuses on the Pharisee's offense at her actions, and on Jesus' sayings about forgiveness. The second is the story of the anointing at Bethany, in the home of Simon the leper, when because of her love for Jesus, a woman anoints Jesus' head with expensive ointment. Matthew and Mark present a fairly simple form of the second story. Luke's core story, on the other hand, is of the first type, but with the addition of details from the second. John, then, appears to have worked primarily with a version

similar to Mark's, but with the sometimes awkward addition of details from Luke's story.

5. Even if she was a prostitute, though, it should be kept in mind that prostitution was virtually the only means by which a woman alone and without private resources could support herself. Though such a woman would herself have been scorned, her place in society was accepted both by her customers (who would have become ritually unclean only until sundown), and apparently by their wives for whom the men's frequenting of prostitutes would have accommodated their own seasons of ritual impurity and perhaps have helped to limit the frequency of their own pregnancies. Although the presence of any woman at such a dinner party was far from an everyday occurrence, the presence of the woman in the banquet hall does not necessarily mean that she had come as a prostitute to ply her trade. Rather, it points to the custom of leaving the doors open during a banquet so that beggars and other poor people could wander in and avail themselves of leftover food. For a Pharisee, such sharing of food would count as part of his almsgiving. (See J. Jeremias, *Jerusalem in the Time of Jesus: An Investigation into Economic and Social Conditions During the New Testament Period,* trans, F. H. Cave and C. H. Cave (Philadelphia: Fortress Press, 1969), 359–76; Schürmann, *Das Lukasevangelium,* 431; W. Grundmann, *Das Evangelium nach Lukas,* 2d ed. [Berlin: Evangelische Verlaganstalt, 1963], 170; G. B. Caird, *The Gospel of St. Luke* [New York: Seabury Press, 1968; London: Cox & Wyman, 1963], 114.)

6. E. Schüssler Fiorenza, "Toward a Feminist Biblical Hermeneutics: Biblical Interpretation and Liberation Theology," in *The Challenge of Liberation Theology: A First World Response,* ed. B. Mahan and L. D. Richesin (Maryknoll, N.Y.: Orbis Books, 1981), 98. See also G. Theissen, "Synoptische Wundergeschichten im Lichte unseres Sprachverhältnisses," *Wissenschaft und Praxis in Kirche und Gesellschaft* 65 (1976): 289–308. For an examination of the series of conflict stories in Mark 2:1—3:6 from the perspective of critical sociology, see E. Stegemann, "From Criticism to Enmity: An Interpretation of Mark 2:1—3:6," in *God of the Lowly,* ed. W. Schottroff and W. Stegemann, trans. M. J. O'Connell (Maryknoll, N.Y.: Orbis Books, 1984), 104–17.

7. The most significant difference is Matthew's expression of the response of the crowd, which suggests that humankind in general (or at least the church) has the authority to declare forgiveness and possibly also to heal. Mark and Luke both keep the attention on Jesus in this response.

8. It is possible but unlikely that the story is from Q. The parable occurs at the end of a block of Q material (Matt. 18:10–22), but it is difficult to imagine why Luke would have omitted this parable if he knew of it. The story in Luke that most closely resembles it is the parable of the Dishonest Steward (Luke 16:1–9), but the stories are too different to warrant the conclusion that they were developed from a common core.

9. The proper way to translate the Greek at this point is unclear. It could mean either "seventy-seven" or "seventy times seven." See the discussion of the Matthean version of this saying in R. E. Brown, K. P. Donfried, and J. Reumann, eds., *Peter in the New Testament* (Minneapolis: Augsburg Publ. House; New York: Paulist Press, 1973), 78–79.

10. The punishment described in Matt. 18:34 and the reference to the sale of the debtor and the debtor's family and possessions may also be part of this exaggeration, for these are contrary to Jewish practice. They may represent the storyteller's effort to get the reader's attention both by means of the inner dynamic of the story and by its colorful details. These details, however, in addition to the reference to a king, may instead point to a Gentile origin of the parable. See W. G. Thompson, *Matthew's Advice to a Divided Community: Mt 17,22–18,35* (Rome: Pontifical Biblical Institute, 1970), 214, 218; Jeremias, *Parables of Jesus,* 211.

11. Crossan (*In Parables,* 105–7) underlines the centrality of the character of the satrap in his outline of the three parallel scenes of the parable. In each scene there are three episodes: the setting (vv. 23–25; v. 28; v. 31), a request for mercy (v. 26; v. 29; vv. 32–33), and a response (v. 27; v. 30; v. 34). The satrap is one of the two principal actors in all but one of these episodes (v. 31).

12. Jeremias (*Parables of Jesus,* 212) observes, however, that the second servant's social status makes his request for additional time as unrealistic as the satrap's, since he also would be unable to pay the money he owed.

13. J. Jeremias, *New Testament Theology: The Proclamation of Jesus,* trans. J. Bowden (New York: Charles Scribner's Sons, 1971), 196; J. Carmignac, *Recherches sur le "Notre Père"* (Paris: Letouzey & Ané, 1969), 396; J. J. Petuchowski and M. Brocke, eds., *The Lord's Prayer and Jewish Liturgy* (New York: Seabury Press, 1978), frontispiece. See also R. E. Brown, "The Pater Noster as an Eschatological Prayer," *TS* 22 (1961): 200.

14. The manuscript evidence indicates that Mark 11:26 is a secondary, scribal addition. In fact, the third edition of *UBSGNT* considers its omission "virtually certain," having given that an "A" rating in the apparatus.

15. With his materialist reading of the concerns about purification underlying the issue of Jesus' table community, Belo (*Materialist Reading of Mark,* 109–10) interprets all of the stories about Jesus' table community with outcasts as incidents of the forgiveness of debts, and as part of a larger cancellation of the debt system on which he sees Palestinian society to be based.

CHAPTER 6. JUBILEE IMAGES INTERWOVEN

1. Although the form of the prayer in both Gospels reflects the theological and liturgical interests of the early church, similarities in form and content between the Lord's Prayer and Jewish prayers suggest that it goes back at least to a Jewish-Christian setting, and perhaps to pre-Christian Judaism,

even to Jesus himself. For example, the form of the prayer as a whole, and especially of its opening petitions, resembles the *Kaddish:* "Exalted and hallowed be his great name in the world which he created according to his will. May he let his kingdom rule in your lifetime and in your days, and in the lifetime of the whole house of Israel, speedily and soon. Praised be his great name from eternity to eternity. And to this say: Amen." The petitions for forgiveness and for bread are similar to the sixth and ninth benedictions of the *Shemoneh 'Esreh,* and the final common petition of the Lord's Prayer echoes one of the major themes of that prayer. See Jeremias, *New Testament Theology,* 198; E. Lohmeyer, *"Our Father": An Introduction to the Lord's Prayer,* trans. J. Bowden (New York: Harper & Row, 1965), 302–4. For discussions of the theological and ethical implications of the Lord's Prayer, see M. H. Crosby, *Thy Will Be Done: Praying the Our Father as Subversive Activity* (Maryknoll, N.Y.: Orbis Books, 1977), and D. M. Shriver, Jr., *The Lord's Prayer: A Way of Life* (Atlanta: John Knox Press, 1983).

2. In both of the common petitions as well as in Matthew's third petition, the verbs are in the passive voice, which probably should be seen as a "divine passive," assuming God as the agent. It is thus God who is being asked to effect the glory, reign, and will that express humankind's deepest longing.

3. A. Deissler, "The Spirit of the Lord's Prayer in the Faith and Worship of the Old Testament," in *The Lord's Prayer and Jewish Liturgy,* ed. Petuchowski and Brocke, 7–8. Note also the combination of the themes of God's sovereignty and of the honor of the divine name in Zech. 14:9.

4. The word for "will" *(to thelēma),* and related words, are among the most common words used in the LXX to translate the Hebrew word *raṣôn,* which is found in the Jubilee text of Isa. 61:2 referring to the "year of God's favor." *Raṣôn* is rendered in the LXX by the following terms: *thelēma* and related words—Pss. 29(30):5–8; 39:8(40:9); 102(103):21; 142(143):10; 144(145):19; Prov. 8:35; 1 Chron. 15:15; Esther 1:8; Dan. (LXX) 8:4; 11:16, 36; *dektos* ("acceptable")—Exod. 28:34(38); Lev. 1:3; 19:5; 22:19–21, 29; 23:11; Deut. 33:16, 23; Prov. 11:1; 12:22; 14:9; 15:8; 16:13; Mal. 2:13; Isa. 49:8; 56:7; 58:5; 60:7; 61:2; Jer. 6:20; *eudokia* ("pleasure")—Pss. 5:12(13); 18:14(19:15); 50:18(51:20); 68:13(69:14); 88:17(89:18); 105(106):4; 144 (145):16.

5. See the discussion of the various interpretations traditionally associated with the petition for bread, and in particular with the adjective *epiousios,* in Brown, "Pater Noster," 195–99. As Brown points out, the reference to "giving bread" is rare in the Gospels. In addition to this petition of the Lord's Prayer, it occurs only in the context of the Last Supper (Matt. 26:26//Mark 14:22//Luke 22:19) and in Jesus' feeding of the multitudes (Matt. 14:19//Mark 6:41//Luke 9:16; Matt. 15:36//Mark 8:6; John 6:32). That the latter incident also had eucharistic connotations in the early church can be seen particularly in the "Bread of Life" discourse associated with it in the Gospel of John.

6. Brown, "Pater Noster," 197–98; Lohmeyer, *"Our Father,"* 158; Carmig-

nac, *Recherches sur le "Notre Père,"* 192, 216–17. Once again, as in the petition for forgiveness, Matthew presents an aorist imperative, which suggests a one-time, decisive event, whereas Luke's present imperative, plus his reference to "each" day instead of to "this" day, points to a continued or repeated action. The two versions of the prayer thus highlight two possible meanings of the petition, namely, as a request for God's eschatological intervention (Matthew) and for God's sustaining presence in the meantime (Luke). The larger context of the prayer, and especially the tone set by the first two (or three) petitions, favors Matthew's as the more original meaning, whereas Luke's can be understood as an adaptation prompted by concern for the ongoing life of the early church.

7. The verb in the common petition is a subjunctive of prohibition (BDF, 172.335; 173.337), and should be understood in keeping with the Semitic causative system of verbs. It would thus mean "cause us not to be led into temptation (or 'into the test')," rather than "do not cause us to be led. . . ." That petition is therefore consonant with the earlier petitions that affirm both God's power and God's saving intent, in which the person who is praying hopes to have a share.

8. One cannot talk about the presence of Jubilee images in the Book of Acts in the same sense as in the Synoptic Gospels. Whereas in the Gospels, Jubilee images point to the declaration of "liberty" and of "good news" encountered by humankind in Jesus' proclamation of God's reign, in Acts the language associated with Jubilee images and texts focuses on the proclamation of or about Jesus himself. The fact that Jubilee texts and images are used in the proclamation about Jesus even without their Jubilee meanings suggests that their link to Jesus predates the early church's confession of Jesus as represented in Acts. Indeed, that association may even go back to traditions stemming from Jesus' own message. On the other hand, in the literature of the church, the christological interpretation of Jubilee images and texts probably predates their reintegration with the remembered stories, teachings, and other traditions stemming from Jesus' ministry. Subsequently, then, those earlier categories and meanings would have found their way back into the church's proclamation as the gospel traditions came together into a fuller picture of the ministry and teaching of Jesus.

9. Jubilee images are distributed among the four sources of the synoptic Gospels as follows:

Mark	*Q*
Matt. 9:1–8//Mark 2:1–12//Luke 5: 17–26	Matt. 5:3–6, 11//Luke 6:20–22
Matt. 19:16–22//Mark 10:17–22// Luke 18:18–23	Matt. 6:9–13//Luke 11:2–4
Matt. 6:14–15//Mark 11:25	Matt. 11:2–6//Luke 7:18–23
Matt. 26:6–13//Mark 14:3–9	Matt. 22:1–10//Luke 14:15–24
	Luke 4:16–30 (?)

M	L
Matt. 18:21–35	Luke 7:36–50
	14:12–14
	16:19–31
	19:1–10

CHAPTER 7. IN CHRIST WE ARE SET FREE

1. While no one can take away the need for each of us to discern where in our own lives the confession of Christ needs to take place in deeds of justice for the poor, we in North America can learn much from representatives of the "church of the poor" in Latin America. For a discussion of the "preferential option of the poor," which has been a hallmark of liberation theology in Latin America since the Medellin and Puebla conferences, see G. Gutiérrez, "Liberation and the Poor: The Puebla Perspective," in *The Power of the Poor in History,* trans. R. R. Barr (Maryknoll, N.Y.: Orbis Books, 1983), 125–65.

Scripture Index

119